Beach
Ball
Books

D0194409

ULTIMATE GUIDE TO
BASKETBALL

By James Buckley, Jr.

Beach Ball Books

Published by Beach Ball Books LLC
www.beachballbooks.com

Produced by Shoreline Publishing Group LLC
Santa Barbara, California
www.shorelinepublishing.com
President/Editorial Director: James Buckley, Jr.
Designed by Tom Carling, www.carlingdesign.com
Funky Facts Master: Blake Dorfman
Copy editor: Jim Gigliotti
Index by Nanette Cardon, IRIS
Illustrations by Mike Arnold, www.arnomation.com

Photo Credits: All interior photos courtesy of AP/Wide World except the following: Corbis: 13, 65; iStock: 6, 37, 42. Diagram on page 43 by Robert Prince.

Library of Congress Cataloging-in-Publication on file with publisher.

ISBN: 978-1-936310-02-9 (paperback)
ISBN: 978-1-936310-13-5 (hardcover)

1 2 3 4 5 6 7 8 9 10 QGT 19 18 17 16 15 14 13 12 11 10

INTRODUCTION

On playgrounds, in gyms, and in driveways around the world, people by the hundreds of millions play and watch basketball. Some studies say that it's the most popular sport in the world! So how can you make sure you have all the latest and greatest info on this awesome sport? Easy! Just keep the turning the pages of this, *The Ultimate Guide to Basketball*!

Basketball has a long and fascinating history in the United States, and it's also played in more than 200 other countries. Whether you play with your pals on the half-court at school or cheer for the awesome superstars of the National Basketball Association, you're part of a world-spanning bucket brigade. This book will help you take your passion for the game even farther!

For instance, we guarantee that your favorite team is in here .... that's because we gave each NBA team its own section. You'll also find cool stuff such as how basketball was invented, how to run the pick-and-roll, and why hoopsters are "cagers"! So call a T.O., gather your fellow B-ballers, find a comfy chair and hoop it up!

CONTENTS

TIPOFF!

Swisssh! Another two (or three!) points! Let's get this basketball party started with a look at the first players, more than a century ago. Basketball had a bit of a wild-and-wooly early history, a far cry from the big-time, international sport it is today.

INSIDE:

Find out why Naismith would be surprised to see a ball do this.

THANKS, DOC

Basketball was born one evening in December, 1891. Compare that to most sports, which took years to develop. There are Egyptian tomb paintings of people hitting a ball with a stick (baseball). Carrying around something and getting knocked down? Been going on for centuries (football). Kicking a ball (soccer)? That happened the first time a caveman kicked a rock away into the ferns! Basketball was different. It was the one-day invention of one man: Dr. James Naismith. He was a Massachusetts YMCA coach and P.E. teacher who needed an activity for snowbound students. A piece of paper on which to write the rules, a pencil (now in a museum), and his idea became a huge part of the sports world.

NAISMITH'S ORIGINAL RULES
(somewhat shortened to fit here)

1 The ball may be thrown in any direction with one or both hands.

2 The ball may be batted in any direction with one or both hands.

3 A player cannot run with the ball. The player must throw it from the spot on which he catches it.

4 The ball must be held by the hands. The arms or body must not be used for holding it.

5 No shouldering, holding, pushing, tripping, or striking in any way the person of an opponent shall be allowed; the first infringement of this rule by any player shall come as a foul, the second shall disqualify him until the next goal is made, or, if there was evident intent to injure the person, for the whole of the game, no substitute allowed.

6 A foul is striking the ball with the fist, violation of Rules 3, 4, and such as described in Rule 5.

7 If either side makes three consecutive fouls it shall count as a goal for the opponents (consecutive means without the opponents in the meantime making a foul).

8 A goal shall be made when the ball is thrown or batted from the grounds into the basket and stays there, providing those defending the goal do no touch or disturb the goal.

9 When the ball goes out of bounds, it shall be thrown into the field of play by the person touching it. He has a right to hold it unmolested for five seconds. In case of a dispute the umpire shall throw it straight into the field. The thrower-in is allowed five seconds; if he holds it longer it shall go to the opponent.

10 The umpire shall be the judge of the men and shall note the fouls and notify the referee when three consecutive fouls have been made. He shall have power to disqualify men according to Rule 5.

11 The referee shall be judge of the ball and shall decide when the ball is in play, in bounds, to which side it belongs, and shall keep the time. He shall decide when a goal has been made and keep account of the goals.

12 The time shall be two 15-minute halves, with five minutes rest between.

13 The side making the most goals in that time shall be declared the winner. In the case of a draw the game may, by agreement of the captains, be continued until another goal is made.

Peachy Keen!

The first game was played on December 21, 1891. Two (empty!) peach baskets were hung at each end of the YMCA gym in Springfield, Massachusetts. Since the bottoms were not removed from the baskets (yet), a ladder was brought out to help get the ball out after each field goal!

EARLY HOOPS
TALES OF THE CAGERS

Basketball grew very quickly. Colleges and clubs found that it was a perfect indoor winter sport. Companies found that it was a great way to keep their employees active (see page 14 for more). By the years after World War I, the game was established as a popular (if not professional . . . more on that later) sport. Here are some stories from the early days of basketball to amuse and surprise you.

College Hoops Along with YMCAs, colleges were among the first to form teams. By 1901, schools in what is now the Ivy League were playing in the first intercollegiate league. Yale won the first "championship," finishing 10–4 in 1901. By World War I (1914–1918), more than 400 colleges had teams.

Jumping? No Way! Until the 1930s, players didn't jump when they shot the ball. They used the "set shot," during which both feet stayed on the ground and both hands were behind the ball. Being tall was not a big advantage, oddly. The game was big on passing and moving and low on scoring. It was often sort of like keep-away. Then guys such as Glen

HOOPS FIRSTS

FIRST BALL: a soccer ball (non-laced rubber balls not used until 1930s)

FIRST FIELD GOAL: made by William Chase, the only score of the first game

FIRST COLLEGE TEAM: probably Yale in the late 1890s

FIRST PRO GAME: an 1896 contest between YMCAs from Brooklyn and Trenton; the players got $15 each!

Roberts figured out that if they jumped while they shot, they'd avoid blocks and be nearer the basket! Roberts was scoring 20 points a game for Emory & Henry College when whole teams rarely scored 20 points. His ideas spread quickly and jumping and height soon played a big part in the game.

Why "Cagers"? Many early games were played not in nice gyms but on dance floors, ballrooms, or theater stages. To keep the players from flying off such platforms, wire mesh was strung around the sides . . . like a cage. Though rope netting was later used, basketball players are still sometimes called "cagers." ▼

KEY RULES CHANGES

The rules didn't stop at 13 (see page 8). Here are some key moments in hoops rules history:

1896: backboards added

1898: dribbling allowed

1908: player ejected after five fouls (now six in the NBA)

1916: person dribbling now also allowed to shoot (!)

1936: no more center jump ball after every basket (a move that really sped up the game!)

(more on page 40)

BARNSTORMERS

Several attempts were made to form pro basketball leagues in the years before and after World War I. The first was the six-team National Basketball League in 1898. None lasted too long, but several of the teams that formed then had long and successful lives. They would barnstorm, or travel around, playing local teams before cheering crowds. Here's a look at some of the most well-known early pro traveling squads:

BUFFALO GERMANS
Starting as a YMCA team, they dominated everyone they played for more than a decade. At a 1904 Olympics demonstration tournament in St. Louis, they won six straight games and the championship. Between 1908 and 1911, the Germans won 111 straight games!

ORIGINAL CELTICS
Creative, innovative, and dominant, the Original Celtics (no relation to today's NBA team of similar name) were the best team of the 1920s. Formed in New York after World War I, they played as many 200 games a year, winning more than 90 percent of the time. The Celtics were champions of the short-lived American Basketball League in 1926 and 1927 before shutting down thanks to money problems.

NEW YORK RENAISSANCE
Known as the Rens, they were the best team in the country in the 1930s, winning 88 games in a row at one point. In 1939, they won 112 of 119 games and also won a national pro hoops tournament. Made up only of African-Americans, the Rens were pioneers, taking the game—and their race—into places it was not often seen.

HARLEM GLOBETROTTERS
Today the 'Trotters are known as the "Clown Princes of Basketball" for their hilarious on-court routines and amazing hoops ability. In their early days, though, they were a serious, Chicago-based team that played to win, not to entertain. In 1940, they won 101 games and the world pro title.

EARLY
WOMEN'S HOOPS

In 1892, a teacher at Smith College, an all-women's school near basketball's birthplace in Massachusetts, started a basketball program for her students. Senda Berenson Abbott was the "mother" of women's hoops! Since women were treated differently in those days, she changed a few of the rules. Here's how her girls played basketball:

Three-part court The court was divided in three sections of equal size. Players were assigned to each section . . . and couldn't leave their section! This was to keep the "delicate" girls from running too much!

No stealing To avoid the rough stuff of men's play, she banned players from trying to snatch the ball from another player. Spoilsport!

Keep it moving! Players could not hold the ball for more than three seconds. (This was before dribbling, remember.)

Somehow, the women's game spread, however. It was one of the only organized sports open to women in those days. Many high schools and colleges created teams (the first? Stanford beat Cal in 1896, 2-1). By 1925, the Amateur Athletic Union had set up a national championship. And by 1938, the three zones were cut to two. In 1971, they finally went full-court. It was about time.

All-American Red Heads

The All-American Red Heads were founded in 1936 by C.M. Olson of Cassville, Missouri. The most successful women's barnstorming team ever, they only played men's teams and by men's rules. Featured in popular magazines and on television, they continued to play up through the mid-1970s.

COMPANY TEAMS

Before pro basketball, top players needed a place to play after college. With company and industrial teams, they found a place on the court—and the office, factory floor, and shop. Companies hired top players and gave them jobs . . . and sneakers. The teams started before World War II. By the years after the war, more than 10,000 companies had created teams at every level. The benefits for the players: They got a regular salary but remained amateurs and could play in the Olympics. The companies got attention for their products and gave their employees something to root for. Teams played in the Amateur Athletic Union, and also the National Industrial Basketball League, which was formed in 1947 to determine national champs. Here are some of the top teams of this era:

South Kansas Stage Lines
Kansas City, Missouri
The moving company's team won the first AAU title in 1935.

Phillips 66ers
Bartlesville, Oklahoma
The oil company had a team that dominated play in the 1940s, 1950s, and early 1960s. They won 11 AAU titles as well as 11 NIBL titles

Peoria Cats
Peoria, Illinois
The tractor maker won five AAU titles in the 1950s.

Other teams in the NIBL included the San Francisco Investors, Los Angeles Fibber McGees & Mollys, and the Milwaukee Harnischfegers.

BEFORE THE
MADNESS

The NCAA Final Four has become one of the biggest events on the national sports calendar, with millions of fans picking their favorites and watching game after game. It wasn't always that way, though. College hoops had a life before the Final Four took over. Here's a look back at the road to the current state of things.

Key Dates in Early College Hoops History

1895

FIRST INTERCOLLEGIATE GAME
Minnesota School of Agriculture 9–Hamline 3

1906

NCAA FOUNDED (SORT OF)
The Intercollegiate Athletic Association of the US (IAAUS) was formed. It changed its name to NCAA four years later.

1926

FIRST WOMEN'S AAU CHAMPIONSHIP
The Pasadena Athletic Club won over a field of six teams.

1938

FIRST NIT
The National Invitational Tournament was held in Milwaukee; Temple University beat the University of Colorado in the final.

1939

**FIRST NCAA
MEN'S BASKETBALL TOURNAMENT**
Oregon beat Ohio State 46–33 in the final game, held in Evanston, Ill.

THE BIRTH OF THE NBA

In the years before World War II, several groups tried to start pro basketball leagues. The only one that stuck around was the National Basketball League (NBL), which began in 1937 and had about a dozen teams. In 1946, the Basketball Association of America was formed with 11 teams to rival the BAA. Two years later, the NBL's four best teams jumped to the BAA; the next year, the rest of the NBL came on board. By 1949, the league had 17 teams and a new name: the National Basketball Association. Most of the teams were in the Northeast and in the Midwest. The team farthest west was in Denver; the farthest south was only in St. Louis! The NBA has come a long way, baby!

FIRST NBA GAME The score was New York Knicks 68–Toronto Huskies 66, in a game played in Toronto!

FIRST NBA BASKET Scored by the Knicks' Ozzie Schectman on November 1, 1946. The NBA includes the stats and seasons from the BAA in its official history.

Earl Lloyd (right)

FIRST NBA SCORING CHAMPION
George Mikan, Lakers–27.4 points per game

THE FIRST NBA CHAMPION
The Minneapolis Lakers, led by star center George Mikan, beat the Syracuse Nationals in six games.

FIRST AFRICAN-AMERICAN IN THE NBA
Hard to believe today, but no black players played pro hoops until 1950. Earl Lloyd played for the Syracuse Nationals that year, along with Sweetwater Clifton of the Knicks. Chuck Cooper played for the Celtics and later for other NBA teams.

THE FIRST SEASON
NBA: 1949-50

EASTERN DIVISION

Syracuse Nationals
New York Knicks
Washington Capitols
Philadelphia Warriors
Baltimore Bullets
Boston Celtics

CENTRAL DIVISION

Rochester Royals
Minneapolis Lakers
Chicago Stags
Fort Wayne Pistons
St. Louis Bombers

WESTERN DIVISION

Indianapolis Olympians
Anderson Packers
Tri-Cities Blackhawks
Sheboygan Red Skins
Waterloo Hawks
Denver Nuggets

EARLY
NBA HEROS

They didn't get the acclaim that Kobe Bryant, LeBron James, and Carmelo Anthony get these days, but the early superstars of the NBA are worth remembering. Without the early success of these Hall of Famers, today's players might not have a league to play in!

◀◀◀ PAUL ARIZIN
Philadelphia Warriors: 1950–62

Not as well known as some of the other players here, Arizin was one of the NBA's best early sharpshooters. He was not the first to use a jump shot, but he was the first to be really successful with it. He led the NBA in scoring twice and was a 10-time All-Star. His career average of 22.8 points per game was one of the highest ever for more than two decades.

BOB COUSY
Boston Celtics: 1950–63

Cousy created the position of point guard. He was the first to use dribbling as a weapon, and his passing set the stage for today's offensive showstoppers. He led the NBA in assists eight times, was a 13-time All-Star, and was the 1957 NBA MVP. His leadership helped the Celtics win their first six NBA titles (on the way to an NBA-record 17 overall).

GEORGE MIKAN
Minneapolis Lakers: 1948–56

The first great big man in the sport, Mikan helped the Lakers win four NBA titles (and three more in the ABA and NBL). He was the first center to use his height to become a top scorer. Mikan was such a big star that a famous billboard once read, "New York Knicks vs. George Mikan." He was also well-known for wearing glasses while he played and for wearing uniform No. 99.

BOB PETTIT
Milwaukee/St. Louis Hawks: 1954–65

Pettit was a terrific all-around player and a top scorer. He was the first NBA player to top 20,000 points in his career. He also won two NBA MVP trophies (1956 and 1959) and two scoring titles. Pettit was also known for a tough, never-quit style of play that made him a fierce rebounder.

BILL SHARMAN
Washington Capitols: 1950–51;
Boston Celtics: 1951–1961

A great shooter while he was moving (he averaged 17.3 points per game), he was even better standing still. Sharman led the NBA a record seven times in free-throw shooting. He teamed with Cousy to establish the backcourt roles still a part of the game today. Sharman was later a successful coach, leading the Lakers to the 1972 NBA title.

Not Playing Anymore

The NBA has not had too many teams stop playing, but there were a few. You're a real hoops nut if you have ever read about these defunct (not playing anymore) teams.

YEARS	TEAM
1947–50	Chicago Stags
1950–53	Indianapolis Olympians
1947–50	St. Louis Bombers
1950	Sheboygan Red Skins
1950	Waterloo (Iowa) Hawks

BOSTON CELTICS

In every one of the NBA's six decades except the 1990s, the Boston Celtics have been NBA champions. Their total of 17 titles (through 2010) is the most in the league, and they have boasted some of the game's greatest heroes.

GAME 1?
1946

The Celtics were one of the first teams in the Basketball Association of America, which merged with the National Basketball League to form the NBA in 1949.

 MAGIC MOMENT
2008 NBA Finals

Lots to choose from, but let's go with the Celtics' most recent title, their first since 1986, breaking their longest title-free streak.

LOWEST LOW
1996–97 Season

The Celtics' sorry 15-win total this season was the lowest in any of the storied franchise' 64 NBA campaigns.

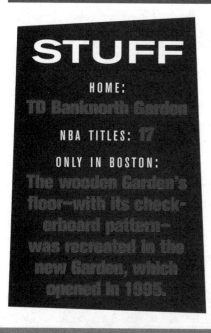

STUFF

HOME:
TD Banknorth Garden

NBA TITLES: 17

ONLY IN BOSTON:
The wooden Garden's floor—with its checkerboard pattern—was recreated in the new Garden, which opened in 1995.

STAR SEASONS!

1957 Led by guard Bob Cousy, the Celtics won their first NBA title, defeating the St. Louis Hawks in seven games.

1981 The rivalry between Boston's Larry Bird and L.A.'s Magic Johnson continued. Bird won this round and Boston won the title.

2008 Kevin Garnett was named the NBA's defensive player of the year.

The Ultimate Celtic

BILL RUSSELL

The greatest rebounder in NBA history was also the greatest champion. Russell's 11 NBA rings are more than twice as many as any other player. His defense and leadership helped the Celtics own the 1960s. For the last two of their titles, he was also the player-coach, the first African-American in U.S. sports to hold that job.

FUNKY FACTS

➜ Boston became the first NBA team to draft an African American player when Chuck Cooper was picked in 1950.

➜ The Celtics have retired 21 uniform numbers, the most in the NBA, including 00 for Robert Parish.

➜ The Celtics won eight consecutive NBA titles from 1959-1966. That's the longest championship streak of any major professional sports team in North America.

➜ Legendary Celtics center Bill Russell holds the record for the most rebounds in a single game. On February 9, 1960, he pulled down a whopping 51 while playing the Syracuse Nationals.

SUPERSTAR! PAUL PIERCE

In his 13th season with Boston, Pierce has been the centerpiece of their most recent NBA titles. His powerful inside scoring game and fiery leadership as captain are the keys to the Celtics success.

➜ The Celtics are the only team in the NBA to have players' names on the back of their warm-up jackets.

You Can Look It Up! BOSTON'S OFFICIAL WEBSITE: www.nba.com/celtics.com

NEW JERSEY NETS

Playing in the shadow of the famous New York Knicks, the Nets have not had nearly as much success, though they did win two ABA titles. A move to Brooklyn in the near future might mean big things for the team.

GAME 1?
1968

The Nets joined the American Basketball Association in 1968 as the Americans. They changed their name to the Nets and joined the NBA in 1977.

👍 MAGIC MOMENT
2002 NBA Finals

The Nets won their first Eastern Conference title and made the NBA Finals. However, they lost there to the Lakers in six games.

👎 LOWEST LOW
2009–10 Season

The Nets couldn't wait for last season to end. They won only 17 games and had the worst record in the entire NBA!

STUFF

HOME:
Barclays Center*

NBA TITLES: 0

ONLY IN BROOKLYN:
The Nets will be the first pro sports team in Brooklyn, New York, since the Dodgers left in 1957.

*Scheduled to open in 2011.

STAR SEASONS!

1975
The mighty Julius "Dr. J" Erving led the ABA in scoring and led the Nets to their first title.

1982
Power forward Buck Williams made the first of three All-Star Game appearances in five seasons, a bright spot in a tough run for the Nets.

2003
Guard Jason Kidd led the NBA in assists, a feat he repeated the following season.

BUCK WILLIAMS

Williams spent the first eight (1981–89) of his 17 NBA seasons with the Nets. His name is all over the team's career record book. He leads in career points, games played, minutes played, free throws, and rebounds. A three-time All-Star with New Jersey, Williams helped the Nets make the playoffs five times.

#1

FUNKY FACTS

➔ The Nets name didn't just come from the basket. They chose it because it rhymed with two other pro teams in the area: the New York Jets and the New York Mets.

➔ In 1977 the Nets became the first team in NBA history to have an all-left-handed starting lineup: Tim Bassett, Al Skinner, Bubbles Hawkins, Dave Wohl, and Kim Hughes.

➔ The Nets' home through the 2010 season was the Prudential Center, located in the Meadowlands in New Jersey.

➔ The Nets mascot is a giant wolf named Sly, who excels at high-flying slam dunks.

SUPERSTAR! BROOK LOPEZ

In only his third season, Lopez has become one of the top young centers in the league. A top rebounder, he sometimes has to play his twin brother Robin, a center with the Suns.

➔ Nets owner, Mikhail Prokhorov of Russia, who bought the team in 2010, is the NBA's wealthiest owner. He's worth an estimated $17 billion.

You Can Look It Up! NEW JERSEY'S OFFICIAL WEBSITE: www.nba.com/nets.com

NEW YORK KNICKS

Though recent seasons have not been kind to them, the Knicks have one of the NBA's famous names, a pair of NBA titles, and one of the most well-known homes in the game. Is more glory ahead for New York's finest?

GAME 1?
1946

New York's entry in the new Basketball Association of America was (and still is) officially known as the Knickerbockers, after the Dutch citizens who founded Manhattan.

👍 MAGIC MOMENT
Reed's Courage

The Knicks won their first NBA title in 1970, thanks to a great backcourt and to the leadership of their center Willis Reed.

👎 LOWEST LOW
0 for 2000s

The once-mighty Knicks had a tough decade. The last time they finished with a winning record was way back in 2001.

STUFF

HOME:
Madison Square Garden

NBA TITLES: 2

ONLY IN N.Y.:
The current Garden on Eighth Ave. is actually the fourth building in New York to have that name.

STAR SEASONS!

1951
In their second NBA season, the Knicks ended up in the NBA Finals, losing to Rochester in seven games.

1985
Bernard King was the last Knick to lead the NBA in scoring, with a 32.9 ppg average.

1985
The Knicks had the first overall pick in the NBA draft and they chose center Patrick Ewing, who led the team for 15 seasons.

The Ultimate Knick

PATRICK EWING

It's tempting to pick an older star like guard Walt Frazier or forward Bill Bradley, but we're going with the Knicks' all-time leader in games, points, rebounds, and even steals! Hall of Famer Patrick Ewing was the center—and the centerpiece—of the Knicks team from his first game to his last with the team in 2000.

#1

FUNKY FACTS

➡ The Knicks are one of just two teams to play in the same city they did when the NBA began in 1946. The other is the Boston Celtics.

➡ Former Knicks great Bill Bradley was accomplished off the court as well. A Rhodes Scholar from Princeton, he later served three terms as a U.S. Senator from New Jersey and ran for President in 2000.

➡ In the 1999 playoffs, the Knicks scored three huge upsets to become the first No. 8 seed to make the NBA Finals, where they lost to the Spurs.

➡ The Knicks welcomed a familiar name for 2011: Patrick

SUPERSTAR!
AMAR'E STOUDEMIRE

Already a five-time All-Star though he's only 27, Stoudemire joined the Knicks in 2010. New York fans hope the big man can lead them to the playoffs. He brings a strong inside game and veteran leadership.

Ewing Jr. follows in his dad's sneakersteps as a Knicks center.

➡ New Knicks star Amar'e Stoudemire's nickname: STAT.

You Can Look It Up! NEW YORK'S OFFICIAL WEBSITE: www.nba.com/knicks.com

PHILADELPHIA 76ERS

It's been a while since Philadelphia brought home a title, but their fans have enjoyed some of the most exciting players in the league, from high-scoring A.I. and Dr. J. to Charles Barkley, the Round Mound of Rebound.

GAME 1?
1950

The 76ers started as the Syracuse Nationals in the NBA's second season. The team moved to the City of Brotherly Love in 1963 and took on its patriotic name.

MAGIC MOMENT
Philly First!

With big Wilt Chamberlain leading the way, the 1967 team won its first title since moving to Philadelphia.

LOWEST LOW
Worst ever

Setting a record no team wants, the 76ers won only 9 games in 1972–73, the fewest ever for a club in a full season. Yuck.

STUFF

HOME:
Wells Fargo Center

NBA TITLES: 3

ONLY IN PHILLY:
The 76ers share their huge arena with the NHL's Flyers, along with concerts, ice skating events, and even the X Games!

STAR SEASONS!

1955 In their sixth season and third trip to the Finals, the team— then in Syracuse—won its first NBA championship.

1983 Big Moses Malone led the NBA in rebounding, was named the MVP, and led the 76ers to the NBA title.

2001 With the first of his two NBA scoring titles, guard Allen Iverson was named the NBA MVP.

The Ultimate 76er

JULIUS ERVING

Other 76ers had more points or played more games. But none brought more fame and flair to the team than Dr. J. One of the greatest dunkers ever, he played the last 11 seasons of his Hall of Fame career in Philly. He was the 1981 NBA MVP and an 11-time All-Star. He was also a two-time All-Star MVP.

#1

FUNKY FACTS

➜ The 76ers ended the Boston's streak of eight straight championships by beating the Celtics in the 1966-67 Eastern Conference finals. During the last game of the series, Philly fans chanted "Boston is dead!"

➜ So how did the 76ers do in 1976? Not bad. In the season that started that year, they made it to the NBA Finals, losing to Portland.

➜ The 2000-01 76ers featured a ton of award hardware: NBA MVP Allen Iverson, Coach of the Year Larry Brown, Defensive Player of the Year Dikembe Mutombo, and Sixth Man of the Year Aaron McKie.

SUPERSTAR! ANDRE IGUODALA

Along with being a solid outside shooter and ballhandler, Iguodala is one of the NBA's iron men. In his first six seasons, he missed only six games!

➜ The 76ers mascot is a giant rabbit named Hip Hop. He uses a trampoline to perform amazing dunks and other tricks at halftime to entertain fans.

You Can Look It Up! PHILLY'S OFFICIAL WEBSITE: www.nba.com/sixers.com

TORONTO
RAPTORS

O Canada! The native home of basketball's inventor got a long-term (see "Game 1") team in 1995 when the Raptors were named as an expansion team. They're still looking for their first title, but they're very much in the hunt.

GAME 1?
1995

The first NBA game was played by in Toronto by the Huskies in 1946. They left in 1947 and the league didn't return to Canada until the Raptors expansion team came in 1995.

👍 MAGIC MOMENT
A Title!

In 2007, the Raptors won their first (and so far, only) Atlantic Division title this year, winning 47 games, third best in the East.

👎 LOWEST LOW
Slow Start

The Raptors won only 16 games in their third NBA season. They were new, right? But two years later, they were in the playoffs.

STUFF

HOME:
Air Canada Centre

NBA TITLES: 0

ONLY IN TORONTO:
Only at Toronto home games is the Canadian National Anthem performed second, in the place of honor.

STAR SEASONS!

1999 Guard Vince Carter got the Raptors their first major award when he was named the NBA Rookie of the Year.

2001 The Raptors won their first-ever play-off series, defeating the Knicks in five games in the Eastern Conference first round.

2010 Forward-center Chris Bosh played in his fifth straight NBA All-Star Game.

The Ultimate Raptor

VINCE CARTER

Chris Bosh is the Toronto career leader in games, but he's on the Heat now, so we'll choose a player who put the Raptors on the map. High-flying Vince Carter earned the nickname Air Canada for his spectacular dunks. Carter's scoring punch gave Toronto its first real superstar, though he has played for two teams since.

#1

FUNKY FACTS

➜ Other names that were considered for the NBA's Toronto team were the Beavers, Dragons, Hogs, Scorpions, T-Rex, Tarantulas, and Terriers.

➜ The team's mascot has a huge red dinosaur head. Named Raptor, not surprisingly, he is fond of "swallowing" fans with his enormous mouth!

➜ The first Canadian picked in the first round of the NBA Draft was Leo Rautins in 1983 by the 76ers.

➜ The 1998-99 Raptors featured five rookies, including a pair of future superstars: 18-year-old Tracy McGrady and his cousin, Vince Carter.

SUPERSTAR!

ANDREA BARGNANI

It's fitting that the NBA's only foreign team sports four players from outside the U.S. One of the best is 7-0 Bargnani, an Italian native who is a powerful inside rebounder and scorer.

➜ After the Vancouver Grizzlies moved to Memphis in 2001, the Raptors became the only Canadian team in the NBA.

You Can Look It Up! TORONTO'S OFFICIAL WEBSITE: www.nba.com/raptors.com

1ST QUARTER

Nuts and bolts. We could say this chapter is about the nuts and bolts of basketball: the ball, the court, the gear, the rules, etc. But you wouldn't want nuts and bolts on the court. The players would trip over them and the metal would scratch the hardwood. So let's just say, these are "Basketball Basics."

INSIDE:

A lonely ball just wants someone to show up and play with it.

THE BALL

The game starts with the ball. The first basketballs were actually soccer balls with laces that held the leather panels together. The laces disappeared by the 1920s, to the delight of dribblers everywhere. Here are some facts about the object known as "the rock."

OFFICIAL SIZE?
An NBA ball is 29.5 inches around and 9 inches across. It weighs 22 ounces. The ball used by the WNBA is about an inch smaller around and weighs 2-4 ounces less.

WHY ORANGE?
Early basketballs were brown like the leather they were made of. They started to be colored orange in about 1958. The Spalding company (possibly inspired by Butler coach Paul Hinkle, though that might be a bit of a myth) tried out a ball that would be easier for players to see in darkish arenas. Orange turned out to work well, so the color stuck. When the American Basketball Association played from 1967–76, it used a red-white-and-blue ball. The WNBA uses a ball that alternates white and orange panels. Of course, you can also buy balls in a variety of colors.

WHY THE PEBBLES?
Leather is too smooth to grab. Without the rough, pebbly texture, the ball would slip out of players' hands. The pebbles make for a better grip.

LEATHER OR RUBBER?
If you're going to only play indoors, use a leather ball. If you're going to play outdoors, too, however, go with rubber. A leather ball will be ruined if you use it on a playground or a driveway. Rubber will work indoors or out. By the way, rubber basketballs were first used in 1942.

THE COURT

Here's a diagram of a basketball court showing the key lines and dimensions. One recent change: In 2010, international basketball switched the shape of its key to match the one used in the NBA. Before, non-U.S. keys were wider under the basket than at the free-throw line. Starting in 2010, all courts will have the rectangular key. Also, the NBA, NCAA, women's, and international hoops each have different distances for the three-point line.

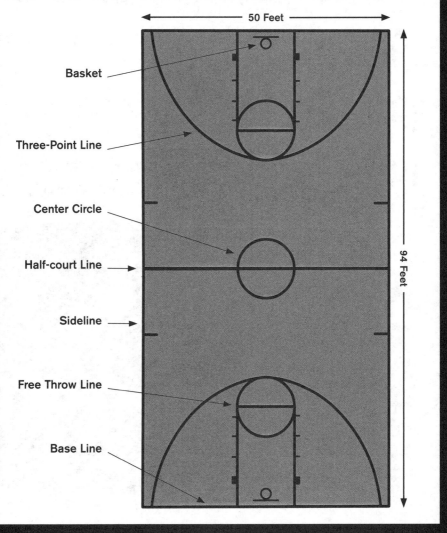

50 Feet

94 Feet

Basket

Three-Point Line

Center Circle

Half-court Line

Sideline

Free Throw Line

Base Line

SNEAKERS!

You can't play basketball in cleats, boots, or snowshoes. You need sneakers—rubber soles to grip the wood or the concrete, canvas or leather tops to support your feet. Shoes like those were actually around for about 30 years before an ad man named Henry Nelson McKinney thought to call them "sneakers." Basketball has done more to spread sneakers around the world than anything else. Here are some of the key dates in the history of sneakers:

1908 A man named Marquis Converse starts a sneaker company that would rule the hoops world for 50 years.

1916 Keds were first made by the Goodyear Rubber Co. They put canvas tops on rubber soles.

1917 The Converse All-Star is the first sneaker made just for hoops. In 1923, it takes on the name of a player-turned-salesman, Chuck Taylor (see box).

CHUCK TAYLOR

The most popular basketball shoe ever was named for this player and salesman. The rubber-soled, canvas-topped shoe was first made in 1921. Taylor joined Converse in 1923 and helped make the shoe better. It was named for him, and he became its most famous salesman. He helped it become the training shoe of the U.S. Army. Anyone who has played hoops has heard of "Chuck Taylors" (worn by all players at right).

1931 Over in Germany, Adi Dassler creates his first rubber-soled tennis shoe for his company, adidas.

1950s Sneakers move from games to the general public, mostly teenagers, especially after movie star James Dean is spotted wearing them.

1962 The company that would become Nike in 1968 is founded by Phil Knight, who first called it Blue Ribbon Sports.

1972 A Nike shoe with a waffle sole becomes a huge hit with runners . . . but not with hoopsters.

AIR JORDAN

Another famous name is attached to the most popular shoe of recent years. In 1985, at the top of his game, Michael Jordan teamed with Nike to introduce Air Jordans. The leather shoes were an immediate hit around the world. Millions were sold to wearers who wanted to "be like Mike." They came first in Chicago Bulls red and black, but have been available in lots of other colors and styles over the years.

1982 Nike introduces the "Air" line, sneakers with air pockets that provide cushion.

1985 Air Jordans, named after Bulls star Michael Jordan (see box), quickly become the most popular sneakers ever. By 2010, more than 25 new styles of Air Jordans had been created.

1989 The Reebok Pump is introduced. The sneaker had a built-in pump so users could inflate their shoes to perfectly fit their feet.

TAKE YOUR
POSITIONS

Basketball teams each have five players on the court. Those five players each play a position based on their skills and what the team needs them to do. These positions are not limited to an area on the court. Instead, all five players play all over the court at both ends. However, the five positions each have special jobs that they do. In early basketball, there were three positions for the five players: center, two forwards, and two guards. In recent times, however, other ways of describing the positions have been added. Here is how the five positions break down today. The numbers with each position name come from the system that most teams use to describe these jobs. (To read about some of the best players at each position, see pages 118–123.)

POINT GUARD (1) This is the quarterback of the team, the leader of the offense. He brings the ball upcourt, makes a lot of passes and assists, and also scores when he can. Point guards are leaders, but they're also great ballhandlers.

SHOOTING GUARD (2) Often a high-scoring player with a great outside shot, the shooting guard also handles the ball well and is involved with passing. He works with the point guard to form the "backcourt" of a team. Both guards are also very tough defenders who must take on the skilled guards of the other team.

SMALL FORWARD (3) They're not really small . . . some small forwards are nearly 6-10! And they score big, not small. Many teams' best player is the small forward. His job is to score from inside and outside, to defend the other team's best shooters, and to get out early on fast breaks. The two forwards and center make up the "frontcourt."

POWER FORWARD (4) Look for this position closer

This shows basically where the positions play, but they all move around.

to the basket. Power forwards contribute rebounds on both ends of the court and close-in scoring on offense. On defense, they have to help the center clog the lane to prevent easy baskets. They are often the biggest or second-biggest players on a team.

CENTER (5) The man in the middle, he's usually the team's tallest player. He uses that height to pull down rebounds as well as score in traffic from under the basket. Centers usually play with their back toward their own basket until a shot is taken. Centers who can pass well can really help a team expand their offensive choices, too. On defense, he sticks with the other team's biggest player and tries to shut him down.

The Sixth Man

Most teams have one key player who is the first one off the bench. He can usually play several positions well (though he is not often a center). Most sixth men are great on defense, can handle the ball, and can hit shots from outside. The NBA gives an award each year to the best sixth man.

TALKIN' HOOPS

You can play basketball and you can watch basketball . . . but can you talk basketball? Here's a rundown on some of the more interesting slang terms that hoopsters use when talking about their games.

ankle-breaker: a move that is so good that the defender trips or gets his feet tangled (not really broken!)

charity stripe: the free-throw line

brick: a really bad shot

bucket: the basket or a successful shot

clean the glass: make a rebound, or "board"; the glass is the backboard

dish: pass the ball with crowd-pleasing style ▼

facial: ▶
a slam dunk performed by flying over or into a defender

go to the hole: drive to the basket

gym rat: a person who spends many hours practicing basketball

my bad: what you say when you make a mistake on the court

paint: the area beneath and in front of the basket formed by the key

rock: the basketball

trey: shorthand for a three-point shot

OLD-TIME TALK

There are a lot of new words in basketball, but most of the old ones are still around, too. Here are a few that you probably don't hear very often, though.

cagers: nickname for basketball players—from the chicken wire that sometimes surrounded early courts

netmen: nickname for basketball players

set shot: a shot made without jumping; the old way to shoot

THE RULES, THEY

The game of basketball is still very much like the game invented by Dr. Naismith more than 100 years ago (page 8). But that doesn't mean it hasn't changed at all. Over the years, new rules and ways of playing have been added. The new rules helped to speed up the game, making it more exciting for fans and players alike. Here's a look at some of the most important changes to the way basketball is played.

◀◀◀The Three-Second Rule
ADDED IN 1936

No offensive player can be inside the key area beneath the basket for more than three seconds. This rule was added to prevent offensive players from "camping out" under the basket. Players can go in to shoot and to get rebounds, but they have to stay outside the key when they're not moving.

The Shot Clock
ADDED IN 1954 (NBA) AND 1985 (NCAA)

This is the big one. In the NBA, a team must take a shot that at least touches the rim within 24 seconds of taking possession of the ball. In the NCAA, it's 35 seconds. Before the rule was put in, a team could simply pass the ball around for as long as it wanted to without shooting (see box). Syracuse Nationals owner Danny Biasone invented the clock in 1954 and it quickly caught on. With the shot clock in place, the game sped up enormously.

ARE A-CHANGIN'

The Three-Point Basket

ADDED IN 1961 (ABL), 1967 (ABA), 1979 (NBA), 1986 (NCAA)

The biggest scoring change in basketball came from outside the NBA. The American Basketball League began play in 1961 to try to challenge the NBA. To attract fans, they added a new way to score: the 3-point shot. A basket made from outside an arc painted on the floor was worth one more point than a regular shot. When the ABA started in 1967, it included the shot. By 1979, the NBA was on board. The three, "from downtown," has added enormous life to basketball, opening up space on offense for everyone, since players now have to defend much farther from the basket. The distances in the NBA, WNBA, and NCAA are each slightly different, but the three-point shot at all levels of the game is basically taken from outside an arc that goes near the sidelines to a point above the top of the key.

Video Replay

ADDED IN 2002 (NBA)

At first, video was used by referees only to see if shots were released before time ended in a half or a game. By 2010, however, it was used to decide whether a shot should count for two or three points, to determine possession after the ball went out of bounds (only in the final two minutes), plus shot clock issues. The referees decide whether to use the replay, and they then look at TV monitors courtside. It came in handy when it had to be used three times in the final 90 seconds of Game 3 of the 2010 NBA Finals.

The Stall and the Four Corners

Before the shot clock, basketball could be really boring. Scores of 10-6 and 13-9 were not uncommon. Some college games even ended 1-0. Because they were not forced to shoot, teams that were in the lead often just played keepaway. They dribbled and passed the ball all around without shooting. If the other team couldn't get the ball, they couldn't catch up. Even into the 1970s, the University of North Carolina was doing this, calling it the Four Corners offense. UNC's style of play was one reason that the NCAA finally added a shot clock in 1985.

BASIC PLAYS

Basketball is a free-flowing game, with players running up and down the court steadily. It looks like everyone's making it up as they go along. But most teams actually are using many well-known plays in each game. Some are called by the coaches, others occur as the ball moves around. If you're a player, you'll know some of these.

Alley-oop

It takes a tall player to grab this high pass. One player passes the ball high and just to the side of the basket. The second, taller player leaps above the defense and snags the ball near the basket and then slams or lays it in.

Bounce pass/Chest pass

These are more techniques than plays, but every player does them. The bounce pass happens when you send the ball to your teammate on one bounce, sometimes avoiding a defender while doing so. A chest pass (pictured) is pushed with both hands from your chest to a teammate's hands.

Pick and roll

A pick or a screen is set when an offensive player blocks a defender from reaching the screener's teammate. As soon as the player with the ball passes the screen, the screener can "roll" toward the basket for a return pass.

Post up

A taller player sets his position at the post—on one side of the key, near the basket. He faces away from the basket so that he blocks his defender. Then the ball is passed to him. He can then spin or jump and try a short shot at the hoop.

Skip pass

This is a great way to reverse the offense. From one side of the basket, a player lofts a pass above everyone's head to a teammate

Plck and roll: X1 dribbles past the screen set by X2, who then rolls and gets the pass.

on the opposite side. By the time the defense moves to cover, that teammate might have an open shot.

THE PLACES
THEY PLAY

Basketball arenas are crowded, noisy places filled with the cheers of fans, the squeak of sneakers on wood, and the thump of the basketball on the floor. Most modern NBA arenas are enormous spaces with room for almost 20,000 people. Some college palaces are that big as well. Here, we pay tribute to the classic hoops homes. These are the places that have seen the greatest moments in the sport, but also are a big part of the game's history. Here are our choices for the most important basketball arenas in the NBA and in the college game.

Allen Fieldhouse
HOME OF **UNIVERSITY OF KANSAS JAYHAWKS**

Opened in 1955 and named for Phog Allen, one of the greatest coaches in college basketball history . . . Kansas has three streaks of 55 or more home wins . . . court itself is named for James Naismith, who was the school's first coach (after inventing the game, too!)

Boston Garden
FORMER HOME OF **THE BOSTON CELTICS**

Known as "The Gahden" to people with a Boston accent . . . opened in 1928, closed in 1995 . . . saw Celtics hang 16 championship banners . . . famous for the checkerboard pattern of its wood floor.

Cameron Indoor Stadium
HOME OF **DUKE UNIVERSITY BLUE DEVILS**

The most famous current college arena . . . home of fans known as "Cameron Crazies" . . . opened in 1940, design puts fans almost on top of the players . . . seats less than 10,000—sounds like twice that!

Dean Dome
HOME OF **UNIVERSITY OF NORTH CAROLINA TAR HEELS**

Officially named for the Tar Heels' longtime coach Dean Smith, its nickname comes from the large, domed roof . . . opened in 1986, it can seat more than 21,000 . . . packed for every UNC game.

The Fabulous Forum
FORMER HOME OF **LOS ANGELES LAKERS**

Opened in 1967, designed to look like the Forum in Rome . . . home

Just say "The Garden," and hoops fans know you mean Madison Square.

to the Lakers and hockey's L.A. Kings until both moved to the Staples Center in downtown L.A. . . . where the Lakers' "Showtime" teams won five NBA titles in the 1980s.

McArthur Court

HOME OF THE **UNIVERSITY OF OREGON DUCKS**

Opened in 1926, "Mac" Court is also known as "The Pit" . . . seats loom over the court so that players feel like they're in a bowl.

Madison Square Garden

HOME OF THE **NEW YORK KNICKS**

Basketball's most famous arena, home to dozens of famous games . . . the current Garden opened in 1968, but is fourth building with that name.

Palestra

HOME OF **THE UNIVERSITY OF PENNSYLVANIA QUAKERS**
AND **ST. JOSEPH'S HAWKS**

A classic old building open in Philadelphia since 1927 . . . once known as the Cathedral of College Basketball . . . claims to have hosted more NCAA regular-season and tournament games than any other arena.

Pauley Pavilion

HOME OF **UCLA BRUINS**

UCLA won nine of its 10 NCAA titles from 1964–1975 . . . Bruins once reeled off 98-game home winning streak.

CHICAGO BULLS

Though he hasn't played for them since 1998, Michael Jordan continues to loom over the Bulls. He carried the team to its only titles and they have been searching for success since he left: Can today's young players do it?

GAME 1?
1966

The Bulls were an expansion team in 1966 and their 33 wins were the best-ever for a first-year team. They made the playoffs eight of their first nine years, too.

MAGIC MOMENT
Finally—Champs

Thanks to the talents of Michael Jordan, the Bulls won their first NBA championship, knocking off the Lakers in five games in 1991.

LOWEST LOW
Life after Mike

Jordan left the Bulls in 1998; in 2001, the team won only 15 games. They didn't return to the playoffs until 2005.

STUFF

HOME:
United Center

NBA TITLES: 6

ONLY IN CHICAGO:
The Matadors are a special group of Bulls fans chosen for their enthusiasm . . . and their very large size!

STAR SEASONS!

1991
In his seventh season, Jordan won his fifth scoring title . . . and the Bulls won the title.

1998
The Bulls won their sixth title of the 1990s, repeating their earlier "threepeat" with back-to-back-to-back crowns.

2007
The Bulls had their best season in the post-Jordan era, reaching the conference semifinals.

The Ultimate Bull

MICHAEL JORDAN

Gee, surprise. The Bulls had never even really gotten close to the top before Jordan arrived in 1984. Over the next decade-plus, Jordan turned the Bulls into six-time champs . . . and himself into a legend. He won six NBA Finals MVPs and led the NBA in scoring 10 times. Since he left, the Bulls have struggled. He's just the best.

#1

FUNKY FACTS

➔ Early Bulls star Jerry Sloan later became the longtime coach of the Utah Jazz, has them to 19 playoff appearances.

➔ The Bulls were the first NBA team to make their starting lineup introductions for home games a big production. They dim the lights, play loud music, and use light shows. The announcer then calls out the team's starters as the fans scream!

➔ Beginning in 1996, the team had a tradition of wearing black socks in playoff games. They broke the tradition in 2009 . . . and it cost them. They lost to the Celtics by 21 points!

➔ Benny the Bull is the team's

SUPERSTAR! DERRICK ROSE

The Bulls made a good choice with the first overall pick in the 2008 NBA Draft. Rose became the Rookie of the Year and a team leader. His all-around skills anchor the Bulls.

popular mascot. He skateboards, slam dunks, and entertains fans with skits. He also plays around with kids and with the Matadors (see "Stuff" at left).

You Can Look It Up! CHICAGO'S OFFICIAL WEBSITE: www.nba.com/bulls.com

CLEVELAND CAVALIERS

LeBron James turned the Cavaliers from also-rans into near-champs . . . but he's gone now. Can the Cavs keep the momentum that his star play brought them? Cavs fans have gotten used to winning . . . have the players?

GAME 1?
1970

The NBA came to Cleveland in 1970, adding the Cavaliers as an expansion team. A "cavalier" is a Spanish word for a knight. The team made the conference finals in its sixth year.

MAGIC MOMENT
Almost!

The Cavs posted the NBA's best record winning a team-record 66 games in 2009. But they were upset in the conference finals.

LOWEST LOW
15 for Four

Cleveland went through four coaches in 1981–82, but even that was not enough, and the team won only 15 games.

STUFF

HOME:
Quicken Loans Arena

NBA TITLES: 0

ONLY IN CLEVELAND:
The upper level of the Cavaliers home court is called Loudville. The fans who sit there are proud of the noise they make!

STAR SEASONS!

1976
Cleveland's Bill Fitch was named the NBA Coach of the Year after leading the team to its first division championship.

1992
Guard Mark Price led the NBA in free-throw percentage for the first of three times.

2008
LeBron James became the first Cavalier to lead the NBA in scoring, averaging 30.0 points per game.

LeBRON JAMES

Current Cavs fans might not like this choice. They think "King James" is sort of a traitor for moving to the Heat for the 2010–11 season. But he's the club's all-time leader in points, shots, free throws, and even steals. His skills also put the team on the map for the first time.

#1

FUNKY FACTS

➜ In the early 1980s, team owner Ted Stepien introduced a polka tune as the team's fight song. It was not popular with the fans, however, and didn't last long. ("Roll out the basketbarrel"?)

➜ Beginning in the 1981-82 season and ending in the 1982-83 season, the Cavs set a record they'd like to give back. Their 24 straight losses are the longest losing streak in NBA history.

➜ Lance Allred became the first deaf player in NBA history when he played for the Cavaliers in 2007.

➜ Cleveland fans did not

SUPERSTAR!

MO WILLIAMS

A quick, talented guard, Williams will have big shoes to fill as he takes over as the Cavs' leader after LeBron James. Williams will bring veteran leadership as well as terrific passing skills.

like the news that superstar LeBron James decided to leave Cleveland and move to the Miami Heat in 2010. Suddenly, lots of his once-popular No. 23 jerseys were turned into rags!

You Can Look It Up! CLEVELAND'S OFFICIAL WEBSITE: www.nba.com/cavaliers.com

DETROIT PISTONS

The Pistons have had three periods of solid play, and fans are hoping for a fourth very soon! The Pistons were playoff regulars in the early days, won a pair of titles in 1989-90, and won again in 2004. When's their next big win?

GAME 1?
1948

The Pistons played their first nine season in Fort Wayne, Indiana. They were part of the NBA's first full season. Moving to Detroit, a car-building center, they kept the name.

MAGIC MOMENT
Pistons Power!

In 1989, led by future Hall of Fame guard Isiah Thomas, the Pistons won their first NBA title, sweeping the Lakers.

LOWEST LOW
They Got Better

Amid a run of six straight losing seasons, 1979–80 was the worst. The Pistons lost a team-record 66 games.

STUFF

HOME:
The Palace

NBA TITLES: 3

ONLY IN DETROIT:
The Pistons have tryouts for fans who want to earn a spot in the Power Plant, reserved for the wildest fans.

STAR SEASONS!

1968 Guard Dave Bing became the only Piston ever to lead the NBA in scoring, pouring in 2,142 points.

1990 Rough-and-tumble forward Dennis Rodman won the first of his two Defensive Player of the Year awards.

2004 The Pistons captured their third NBA title, surprising many by beating the Lakers.

ISIAH THOMAS

Playing his entire 13-year Hall of Fame career in Detroit, Thomas became the team's career leader in points, steals, assists, free throws, and minutes played. He guided the "Bad Boys" of Detroit to two NBA titles and also earned a pair of All-Star Game MVPs. At 6-1, he was never the biggest player, but he had the biggest heart.

FUNKY FACTS

➔ The Pistons got their name from founder Fred Zollner's business in Fort Wayne, which made pistons for car engines.

➔ Before the creation of the shot-clock in 1954, the Fort Wayne Pistons beat the Minneapolis Lakers 19-18 in a 1950 game. It was the lowest scoring NBA contest ever.

➔ The Pistons also hold the record for the most points scored in a game (including overtime) with 186 against the Denver Nuggets in 1983.

➔ Detroit guard Dave Bing was the 1967 NBA Rookie of the Year. In 2009, he was elected the mayor of Detroit.

SUPERSTAR! RICHARD HAMILTON

"Rip," as he is known, is a talented shooter and fierce rebounder. He's also well-known for the plastic mask he wears to protect once-broken bones in his face.

➔ Richard Hamilton is the only player in NBA history to lead his team in scoring without making a single field-goal. On January 6, 2005, Hamilton was 0–10 from the field but 14–14 from the free-throw line.

You Can Look It Up! DETROIT'S OFFICIAL WEBSITE: www.nba.com/pistons.com

INDIANA PACERS

In a basketball-crazy state (Indianans looove their high school and college hoops), the Pacers know they have a lot of fans. They've come very close often, but are still waiting to bring home their first NBA title.

GAME 1?
1967

The Pacers were one of the teams in the first season of the American Basketball Association. They became one of the ABA's best, and joined the NBA in 1976.

👍 MAGIC MOMENT
Early Success

With a victory in the 1973 ABA Finals, the Pacers became the only team to win three titles in the young league.

👎 LOWEST LOW
1982–83

Amid a five-year losing streak, the Pacers set a team record they'd like to give back: winning only 20 games this season.

STUFF

HOME:
Conseco Fieldhouse

NBA TITLES: 0

ONLY IN INDIANA:
The Pacers' mascot is a giant blue cat named Boomer. He speeds around the court on a "go-cat-cart."

STAR SEASONS!

1969 Rebounding ace Mel Daniels won the first of his two ABA MVP awards.

1975 George "The Iceman" McGinnis led the ABA in scoring with a 29.8 ppg average.

2005 Reggie Miller, one of the best pure shooters ever in the NBA, led the NBA in free-throw percentage, the last of five times he would accomplish that.

REGGIE MILLER

No one could shoot the three like Reggie Miller. His amazing skill "from downtown" made him an Indiana favorite and the NBA's career leader in three-point field goals, with 2,560. A five-time All-Star, he is Indiana's all-time leader in points, assists, steals, and smiles created.

#1

FUNKY FACTS

➔ The Pacers were not the first NBA teams from Indy. The Jets played in 1948–49, while the Olympians were in the league for four years, from 1950 through 1953.

➔ A last-second basket by Rik Smits that won Game 4 of the Conference Finals in 1995 is still rememebered today as the "Memorial Day Miracle."

➔ Hoops fans in the "Hoosier State" were thrilled when former Indiana high school and college legend Larry Bird (he was pretty good in the NBA, too) coached the Pacers from 1997–2000. Bird, who also helped out in the front office, led them to the 2000 NBA Finals.

SUPERSTAR! DANNY GRANGER

A big forward at 6-8, Granger nonetheless excels from the outside. Three times, he's been in the NBA top 10 in 3-point field goals. He has led the Pacers in scoring three times, too.

➔ Pacers star Danny Granger says that his favorite movie is *The Dark Knight*, a flick about Batman. However, Granger also says he's afraid of bats!

You Can Look It Up! INDIANA'S OFFICIAL WEBSITE: www.nba.com/pacers.com

MILWAUKEE BUCKS

Milwaukee started strong, winning a title in its third season and finishing as runners-up in their sixth. Since then? Well, not so much. They've had very few superstars and have won only two playoff series since 1989.

GAME 1?
1968

The Bucks joined the NBA as an expansion team in 1969, and by their third season they were NBA champs—the fastest title ever by a new team in the league.

 ## MAGIC MOMENT
1971 NBA Finals

Led by the amazing Kareem Abdul-Jabbar, the Bucks knocked off the Baltimore Bullets to win their first and only NBA title.

LOWEST LOW
A Bad Patch

The Bucks have had bad seasons, but only a few awful ones. The worst came in 1993–94, when they lost 62 games.

STUFF

HOME:
Bradley Center

NBA TITLES: 1

ONLY IN MILWAUKEE:
Inspired by Australian star Andrew Bogut, fans in "Squad 6" cheer the whole game while wearing wigs and sombreros.

STAR SEASONS!

1983 Sidney Moncrief of the Bucks was named the first winner of the new Defensive Player of the Year award.

1986 The Bucks won the Central Division for the seventh straight season, and made it all the way to the Eastern Conference finals.

2010 Center Andrew Bogut finished second in the NBA with a 98.1 defensive rating.

The Ultimate Buck

KAREEM ABDUL-JABBAR

Yes, he spent most of his Hall of Fame career with the Lakers. But Kareem played his first six seasons with the Bucks, won three NBA MVP awards with them, and remains the franchise's all-time leader in points and rebounds. He also led the team to its only NBA championship in 1971.

#1

FUNKY FACTS

➔ The Bucks' high-flying mascot, Bango (a basketball-loving deer who got his name from beloved announcer Eddie Doucette) once did a backflip slam dunk after flying off a 16-foot tall ladder!

➔ There have been seven Dutch players in NBA history and two are Bucks centers: Francisco Elson and Dan Gadzuric.

➔ The Bucks' home court, the Bradley Center, is the home of five sports teams: the Bucks, the International Hockey League's Milwaukee Admirals, the Marquette University Golden Eagles men's basketball team, the NPSL Milwaukee Wave indoor soccer team, and the AFL Milwaukee Mustangs arena football team.

SUPERSTAR!
ANDREW BOGUT

The top pick of the 2005 draft, this big Australian center has become one of the best defensive players in the NBA. He made the All-NBA third team in 2010 and fills the lane like few other players.

You Can Look It Up! MILWAUKEE'S OFFICIAL WEBSITE: www.nba.com/bucks.com

2ND QUARTER

Basketball games put up bigger scoring numbers than any other major sport. Can you imagine a baseball game that ended 104–98? In this section, we look at all sorts of scoring feats and more.

Kareem Abdul-Jabbar shows off his record-setting sky hook.

POINTS GALORE!

The whole point of the game, of course, is to score points. Lots of them! Here are the top 10 scorers in NBA history. All of the totals are through the 2009–2010 season. (PS: Kobe's No. 12 . . . less than 1,000 points out of the top 10!)

PLAYER (YEARS)	POINTS
Kareem **Abdul-Jabbar** (1969–89)	**38,387**
Karl **Malone** (1985–2004)	**36,928**
Michael **Jordan** (1984–2003)	**32,292**
Wilt **Chamberlain** (1959–1973)	**31,419**
Shaquille **O'Neal** (1992–)	**28,255**
Moses **Malone** (1974–1995)	**27,409**
Elvin **Hayes** (1968–1984)	**27,313**
Hakeem **Olajuwon** (1984–2002)	**26,946**
Oscar **Robertson** (1960–1974)	**26,710**
Dominique **Wilkins** (1982–1999)	**26,668**

ABA LEADERS

The ABA had its own scoring leaders during its 10-year history. Here are the top three:

LOUIE **DAMPIER**	13,726
DAN **ISSEL**	12,823
RON **BOONE**	12,153

 58 SECOND QUARTER

SCORE FOR
SCHOOL!

With so many superstars leaving college early to jump to the NBA, the NCAA scoring record of "Pistol" Pete Maravich seems safe. If you score that many points in the college game, you're probably not going to stick around to break any records—not when there's a big paycheck waiting for you in the NBA. Here are the 10 players who scored the most points in their college careers, listed with their schools and the final season they played in (most played four seasons).

POINTS, PLAYER/SCHOOL (FINAL YEAR)

3,667 PETE **MARAVICH**
LSU (1970)

3,249 FREEMAN **WILLIAMS**
Portland St. (1978)

3,217 LIONEL **SIMMONS**
La Salle (1990)

3,165 ALPHONSO **FORD**
Mississippi Valley State (1993)

3,066 HARRY **KELLY**
Texas Southern (1983)

3,058 KEYDREN **CLARK**
St. Peter's (2006)

3,008 HERSEY **HAWKINS**
Bradley (1988)

2,973 OSCAR **ROBERTSON**
Cincinnati (1960)

2,951 DANNY **MANNING**
Kansas (1988)

2,914 ALFREDRICK **HUGHES**
Loyola, Ill. (1985)

MORE ABOUT
THE SCORE

Put together all the points scored by the guys on the previous pages and you've got . . . a pile of points. But those are just single guys. They can only score so much. Let's look at some of the most high-flying, points-scoring, scoreboard-busting teams and games of all time.

126.5
HIGHEST SINGLE-SEASON AVERAGE, POINTS PER GAME: NBA
Denver Nuggets, 1981-82

122.4
HIGHEST SINGLE-SEASON AVERAGE, POINTS PER GAME: NCAA
Loyola Marymount University averaged that total in the 1989-1990 season.

370
MOST TOTAL POINTS IN A GAME: NBA
The Detroit Pistons beat Denver 186–184 in a game that took three overtimes to finish on December 13, 1983.

331
MOST TOTAL POINTS IN A GAME: NCAA
In January of 1989 LMU beat U.S. International 181–150.

304
HIGHEST-SCORING NBA PLAYOFF GAME
The Portland Trailblazers squeaked by the Phoenix Suns, 153–151, in double overtime on May 11, 1992.

264

HIGHEST-SCORING NCAA TOURNAMENT GAME

Loyola Marymount (there they go again!) beat Michigan 149–115 in a 1990 tournament game.

10,371

MOST POINTS BY A TEAM IN AN NBA SEASON

Denver Nuggets poured in a per-game average of 126.5 points over their 82-game 1981–82 season.

4,012

MOST POINTS BY A SCHOOL IN A SEASON (NCAA DIVISION I)

Oklahoma ended its 39 games "sooner" (get it?) in 1988 when they scored an all-time record number of points.

135

MOST POINTS IN A HIGH SCHOOL GAME

More than 50 years after he set the record in 1960, Danny Heater's 135 points for Burnside (W.V.) High still is the most ever.

Hank Gathers and Bo Kimble of the high-scoring 1990 LMU team

THREE-POINT

The three-point play revolutionized basketball. By making a long-range shot worth 33 percent more than a shot from closer to the basket, basketball rulesmakers helped to spread the game farther from the basket. Scoring soared,

NBA

Reggie Miller

PLAYER	THREE-POINTERS*
Reggie **Miller**	2,560
Ray **Allen**	2,444
Dale **Ellis**	1,719
Peja **Stojakovic**	1,703
Jason **Kidd**	1,662
Chauncey **Billups**	1,589
Rashard **Lewis**	1,587
Glen **Rice**	1,559
Eddie **Jones**	1,546
Tim **Hardaway**	1,542
Nick **Van Exel**	1,528
Jason **Terry**	1,523

*Through 2009–10

Ray Allen

SCORING STARS

especially by guys who could hit that long-range jumper. Here are the players who took the most advantage of the new rule and hit the most career three-point shots. The NBA totals are since 1979, while the NCAA shooters date to 1986.

NCAA

PLAYER, SCHOOL	THREE-POINTERS*
J.J. **Redick**, DUKE	457 ▶▶▶
David **Holston**, CHICAGO ST.	450
Keydren **Clark**, ST. PETER'S	435
Chris **Lofton**, TENNESSEE	431
Stephen **Curry**, DAVIDSON	414
Curtis **Staples**, VIRGINIA	413
Jack **Leasure**, COASTAL CAROLINA	411
Keith **Veney**, LAMAR/MARSHALL	409
Doug **Day**, RADFORD	401
Gerry **McNamara**, SYRACUSE	400
Michael **Watson**, UMKC	391
A.J. **Abrams**, TEXAS	389

*Through 2009–10

TRIPLE DOUBLES

Doubles means double figures (10 and up). Triple means three at once. A player earns an unofficial triple double when he hits double figures in three or more stat categories in one game. Most of the time, that means points, rebounds, and assists. Some players swap out blocks or steals for assists. They're pretty rare these days, with only a handful of players able to achieve them. (Only one has had 20 or more in three categories. Wilt Chamberlain had 22 points, 25 rebounds, and 21 assists in a 1968 game.) Here some of the best at putting up triple doubles, through the end of the 2009–10 season.

All-Time Best

PLAYER (YEARS)		TRIPLE DOUBLES
Oscar ROBERTSON	(1960–74)	181
Magic JOHNSON	(1979–96)	138
Jason KIDD	(1994–)	105
Wilt CHAMBERLAIN	(1959–73)	78
Larry BIRD	(1979–92)	59

Currently Playing

Player	Triple Doubles
Jason KIDD	105
LeBron JAMES	34
Grant HILL	29
Kevin GARNETT	16
Kobe BRYANT	16

THE BIG O

Oscar "The Big O" Robertson was one of the best all-around players in NBA history. In 1962, he did something no other player has done: He had a triple double for a season! Per game, he averaged 30.8 points, 12.5 rebounds, and 11.4 assists (one of seven times he led the NBA in that category).

CHARITY STRIPERS

Following many NBA fouls, the player who is fouled gets a free-throw shot. He stands 15 feet from the net, unguarded, and tries to make a one-point shot. Of course, he might also have 15,000 people screaming at the top of their lungs for him to miss. Making free throws can be the difference between a champion and a team going home early. Here are some free-throw wizards:

HIGHEST CAREER PCT.
ALL-TIME: **Mark Price, .9039**
ACTIVE PLAYERS: **Steve Nash, .9033**

MOST CAREER FREE THROWS
ALL-TIME: **Karl Malone, 9,787**
ACTIVE PLAYERS: **Kobe Bryant, 6,543**

CONSECUTIVE FREE THROWS MADE
97, Michael Williams, 1993

MOST FREE THROWS MADE IN A GAME
28, Wilt Chamberlain, Warriors, 1962
28, Adrian Dantley, Jazz, 1984

WORST CAREER PCT.*
Ben Wallace, .417

*Min. 1,000 attempts

BIG GAMES!

TOP 10 SINGLE-GAME SCORING: NBA

POINTS	PLAYER, TEAM	DATE
100	**Wilt Chamberlain,** Warriors	3/2/62
81	**Kobe Bryant,** Lakers	1/22/06
78	**Wilt Chamberlain,** Warriors	12/8/61
73	**David Thompson,** Nuggets	4/9/78
73	**Wilt Chamberlain,** Warriors	11/16/62
73	**Wilt Chamberlain,** Warriors	1/13/62
72	**Wilt Chamberlain,** Warriors	3/11/62
71	**David Robinson,** Spurs	4/24/94
71	**Elgin Baylor,** Lakers	11/15/60
70	**Wilt Chamberlain,** Warriors	3/10/63

Notice one name dominates this list: Wilt "The Stilt" Chamberlain. His greatest night came in, of all places, Hershey, Penn. The Philadelphia Warriors played there to help generate a little love from fans in other parts of the Keystone State. Wilt got off to a hot start . . . and just kept getting hotter. Making an all-time record 28 free throws (and he was normally a bad free-throw shooter), "The Stilt" poured in point after point after point. By halftime, he had 41. After three quarters, he had reached 69. Finally, with 46 seconds left, he did it. Chamberlain became the first and still only NBA player with 100 points in a game.

Pouring on the points . . . filling the bucket . . . lighting up the scoreboard: However you say it, watching one player simply dominate a basketball game can be a thrilling experience. Here are the best single-game performances ever.

TOP SINGLE-GAME SCORING: NCAA

POINTS	PLAYER, SCHOOL	DATE
72	**Kevin Bradshaw,** Alliant Intl.	1/5/91
69	**Pete Maravich,** LSU	2/7/70
68	**Calvin Murphy,** Niagara	12/7/68
66	**Jay Handlan,** Wash. & Lee	2/17/51
66	**Pete Maravich,** LSU	2/10/69
66	**Anthony Roberts,** Oral Roberts	2/19/77
65	**Anthony Roberts,** Oral Roberts	3/9/77
65	**Scott Hafner,** Evansville	2/18/89
64	**Pete Maravich,** LSU	2/21/70

Pistol Pete

The only name on this list three times is that of "Pistol" Pete Maravich, who is the all-time leading scorer in NCAA history, as well as the owner of the three highest single-season points-per-game averages. The player who never met a shot he didn't like to take starred for LSU from 1968-70. With his famous floppy socks and flippy hair, Maravich electrified fans and opponents alike with dazzling ball-handling and an ability to score from outside and inside. He played 10 years in the NBA, winning one scoring title, and was named to the Hall of Fame. Sadly, he died of a heart attack at only 40 in 1988 . . . while playing hoops.

NICKNAMES

Basketball, like other sports, has a very colorful language all its own. That includes the nicknames that players earn. Here's a look at some of the most well-known nicknames from players past and present.

Former Players

REAL NAME	NICKNAME
Charles Barkley	The Round Mound of Rebound
Julius Erving	Dr. J
George Gervin	Iceman
Earvin Johnson	Magic
Michael Jordan	Air Jordan
Karl Malone	The Mailman
Dominique Wilkins	The Human Highlight Film

Current Players

REAL NAME	NICKNAME
Kobe Bryant	Black Mamba
Vince Carter	Vinsanity
Glen Davis	Big Baby
Robert Horry	Big Shot Bob
Allen Iverson	The Answer
LeBron James	The King
Shaquille O'Neal	Shaq Daddy, the Big Aristotle, the Diesel, etc.

GO, GO, GOPHERS!

Colleges have terrific names for their sports teams. We could include the mascots and nicknames of some really small and not-really basketball-famous colleges here, such as the Trinity Christian Trolls, the UC Santa Cruz Banana Slugs, the Webster Gorlocks, and Oglethorpe Stormy Petrels. But we decided to include some strange school names from teams that you might actually have heard of! Here are some of the more unusual school mascot names in college hoops:

Albany Great Danes

Akron Zips

Kent State Golden Flashes

Maryland Terrapins

Minnesota Golden Gophers

St. John's Red Storm

Tulsa Golden Hurricane

Wake Forest Demon Deacons

Wichita State Shockers

ATLANTA HAWKS

The Hawks have landed in several cities, but have only been champions in one of them. Though they have boasted some amazing athletes, the team hasn't been to a conference final since 1961. Keep flying, Hawks!

GAME 1?
1946

Homes of the Hawks: the Buffalo Bison, 1946–49; Tri-Cities Blackhawks, '49-51; as the Hawks in Milwaukee, '51-55; St. Louis, '55-68; and Atlanta since 1968.

👍 MAGIC MOMENT
Long Time Ago

In a different city and a different millennium, the team won its only NBA title in 1958, while playing as the St. Louis Hawks.

👎 LOWEST LOW
2004–05 Season

Amid a nine-year streak of losing seasons (1999–2008), 2004–05 was a low point, as the Hawks lost 69 games.

STUFF

HOME:
Philips Arena

NBA TITLES: 1

ONLY IN ATLANTA:
Before games, fans are treated to an arena-swooping show by Spirit, the team's live hawk mascot.

STAR SEASONS!

1956
In this season, the NBA MVP award was given for the first time. The winner was the great Hawks forward Bob Pettit. He won again in 1959.

2000
Center Dikembe Mutumbo led the NBA in rebounding this season and the next.

2010
With a playoff berth and 53 wins, the Hawks had their best season since 1997.

The Ultimate Hawk

DOMINIQUE WILKINS

Thanks to his amazing leaping ability and creative dunks, Wilkins had one of the NBA's best nicknames: The Human Highlight Film. He was an all-around great player, however, and ended his Hall of Fame career as the Hawks career leader in points, games, and minutes. (A special mention of all-time great Bob Pettit, too.)

FUNKY FACTS

→ What were the Tri-Cities, where the Hawks first played? It's a mix of Rock Island and Moline, Illinois, and Davenport, Iowa.

→ The Hawks traded for All-Star forward Rasheed Wallace in 2004. In his first game with Atlanta, he scored 20 points. His time as a Hawk was short though—he was traded right after the game!

→ In the late 1990s, while their arena was being built, the Hawks played some of their home games in the Gerogia Dome, where the NFL's Falcons play. On March 27, 1998, an NBA-record 62,046 fans watched the Bulls beat the Hawks.

SUPERSTAR!

JOE JOHNSON

Veteran guard Johnson has been a team leader for the Hawks since joining them in his fifth NBA season in 2005. He has averaged at least 20 points per game every season in Atlanta.

→ Before a 2009 playoff game, Spirit, the team's live hawk mascot, decided he wanted a birds-eye view. Instead of returning to his trainer, he perched on the backboard. The game was delayed while he was coaxed down from his new "seat."

You Can Look It Up! ATLANTA'S OFFICIAL WEBSITE: www.nba.com/hawks.com

CHARLOTTE
BOBCATS

The Bobcats' best player is the team chairman. Okay, not really, but when the great Michael Jordan took over control of the team in 2006, he sent a jolt of hoops electricity all over this basketball-crazy state.

GAME 1?
2004

After the Hornets left in 2002, a new Charlotte expansion team was awarded in 2005 to Robert Johnson, who became the first African-American NBA team owner.

MAGIC MOMENT
The Best Yet

In 2009–10, the Bobcats finished with their first winning record ever, and also made the playoffs for the first time.

LOWEST LOW
A Slow Start

Like many expansion teams, the Bobcats struggled in their first season. The team won only 18 games in 2004–05.

STUFF

HOME:
Time Warner
Cable Arena

NBA TITLES: 0

ONLY IN CHARLOTTE:
The Bobcats' home boasts the largest video screen in the NBA, at more than 38 feet high.

STAR SEASONS!

2005 In its first season, Charlotte won its first big award, thanks to NBA Rookie of the Year Emeka Okafor.

2006 Fast-fingered guard Gerald Wallace was the NBA's best thief, leading the league with 2.51 steals per game.

2008 In his only season with Charlotte, Jason Richardson led the NBA in three-pointers.

The Ultimate Bobcat

GERALD WALLACE

After being chosen in the expansion draft, Wallace has been a starter since the Bobcats' first game in 2004. He's the team career leader in everything from games and minutes to steals and total points. In 2009–10, the 6-7 forward averaged the first double-double in Bobcats history, with 10 rebounds and 18.2 points per game.

FUNKY FACTS

→ When Charlotte was awarded its new franchise, fan voting helped narrow the name choices down to this final three: Bobcats, Flight, and Dragons.

→ Center Primoz Brezec, who played for Charlotte in its opening season, was the second NBA player ever from Slovenia.

→ The Bobcats mascot is not a bobcat. He's a related cat named Rufus the Lynx. Tall and very red, he sports snappy sunglasses and often rides around the court on special roller skates.

→ When Larry Brown took over as coach of the Bobcats in 2009, it marked the 10th team

SUPERSTAR!

STEPHEN JACKSON

In his 13th NBA season and with his sixth NBA team, Jackson enjoyed his move to Charlotte in 2009. He posted career highs in both assists and points per game, plus gave a young team a new leader.

that he has led in his 31-year NBA coaching career that started with Carolina in the ABA back in 1972. The former NBA guard led Detroit to the 2004 NBA championship.

You Can Look It Up! CHARLOTTE'S OFFICIAL WEBSITE: www.nba.com/bobcats.com

MIAMI HEAT

The Heat have one NBA title in their short history, but their best years might be ahead, now that they boast one of the greatest trios of players ever to be on one team: Dwyane Wade, Chris Bosh, and LeBron James. Wow.

GAME 1?
1988

Miami was awarded an expansion team to start play in the 1988–89 season. A couple of teams had played briefly in Florida in the ABA and NBA in the late 1960s.

👍 MAGIC MOMENT
2006 NBA Finals

The Heat, led by Dwyane Wade, won their only NBA title after coach Pat Riley returned to the bench midseason.

👎 LOWEST LOW
Very Slow Start

The Heat lost an NBA-record 17 games to start their first season before recording their first win— they won only 14 more that year.

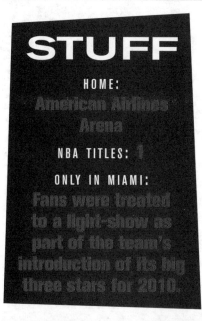

STUFF

HOME:
American Airlines Arena

NBA TITLES: 1

ONLY IN MIAMI:
Fans were treated to a light-show as part of the team's introduction of its big three stars for 2010.

STAR SEASONS!

1997
In its ninth season, the Heat had its best result yet, making it to the Eastern Conference Finals.

2005
Big center Shaquille O'Neal led the NBA in field-goal percentage (he did it again in 2006 while helping the Heat win it all).

2007
Jason Kapono was the most accurate three-point shooter in the NBA this year.

The Ultimate Heat

DWYANE WADE

Heading into his eighth NBA season, all spent in Miami, the man known as "D-Wade" is the face of the franchise. He's also the team's all-time leader in assists, steals, and points (and he was the NBA scoring leader in 2009). A two-time All-NBA selection, he is also a six-time All-Star (and was the MVP of the 2010 game).

FUNKY FACTS

➔ The entry of a woman named Stephanie Freed won a contest that named the Heat.

➔ A.C. Green played in the most consecutive games in NBA history: 1,192 straight games played from 1986–2001. He played the last of his 16 seasons with the Heat.

➔ In 2009, Dwyane Wade became the first player in NBA history to accumulate 2,000 points, 500 assists, 100 steals, and 100 blocks in a season!"

➔ The Heat are one of only four NBA teams whose name doesn't end in an s. The other three are the Utah Jazz, Orlando Magic, and Oklahoma City Thunder.

SUPERSTAR! LEBRON JAMES

The King is in Miami! The man some call the best overall player in the NBA joined the Heat in the 2010–11 season. A two-time NBA MVP, he led the NBA in scoring in 2008.

➔ Miami's head coach as of 2010, Erik Spoelstra, is the first Filipino-American head coach in the NBA as well as the first Filipino-American head coach of any North American pro team.

You Can Look It Up! MIAMI'S OFFICIAL WEBSITE: www.nba.com/heat.com

ORLANDO MAGIC

In its 21 NBA season, the Magic has made the playoffs more often than not, though it hasn't captured the NBA title . . . yet. As the "other" NBA team in Florida, Orlando is ready to make the magic happen!

GAME 1?
1989

The second expansion team given to the Sunshine State, the Magic started slowly, but by its sixth season, it had made it all the way to the NBA Finals.

👍 MAGIC MOMENT
On a Roll

In the 2008-09 and 2009–10 seasons, the Magic won a team-record 59 games each year. They made the 2009 Finals.

👎 LOWEST LOW
Big Comedown

After three straight playoff berths, the Magic plunged in 2003–04, cutting their wins from 42 to 21.

STUFF

HOME:

Amway Arena

NBA TITLES: 0

ONLY IN ORLANDO:

The Dunking Dancers use trampolines and gymnastics to make amazing dunks to entertain fans at halftime.

STAR SEASONS!

1995 On the way to their first NBA Finals, the Magic enjoyed the leadership of Shaquille O'Neal, the NBA scoring leader with a 29.3 points per game average.

2004 The great forward Tracy "T-Mac" McGrady won the first of his two straight NBA scoring titles.

2008 Dwight "Superman" Howard led the NBA in rebounding.

NICK ANDERSON

A part of the Magic for its first 10 seasons, Anderson is the team's all-time leader in points, games, minutes played, and steals. A versatile player who saw time at forward and guard, he was one of the league's top three-point shooters, too. He wrapped up his NBA career with the Kings and the Grizzlies.

#1

FUNKY FACTS

➜ The team was almost called the Challengers, in tribute to nearby NASA's space shuttles. But a special panel of folks ended up choosing the name. Oh, did we mention that Disney World, the "Magic Kingdom" is also in Orlando?

➜ When he was with the Magic in 1993, a young Shaquille O'Neal also began a rap singing career. His first album, *Shaq Diesel*, was certified platinum for selling a million copies!

➜ The Magic's home court is officially the Amway Arena, but people call it the "O-rena" in a tribute to the city of Orlando.

SUPERSTAR!
DWIGHT HOWARD

Superstar? This is Superman! That's the nickname for this all-around talent, who not only pours in points, but is one of the NBA's fiercest defenders and a three-time NBA rebounding leader.

➜ Star center Dwight "Superman" Howard loves to do impersonations, and two of his favorites are actor/governor Arnold Schwarzenegger and his coach, Stan Van Gundy.

You Can Look It Up! ORLANDO'S OFFICIAL WEBSITE: www.nba.com/magic.com

WASHINGTON WIZARDS

A well-traveled franchise, the team that is the Wizards today has been known by five other names in nearly 50 years. They've only been known as "NBA Champions" once in all those years, however.

GAME 1?
1961

The Chicago Packers played for one year, then became the Zephyrs for another, then moved to Baltimore in 1963. It was on to D.C. in 1973; the Wizards' name came in '97.

👍 MAGIC MOMENT
Champions!

The 1978 team then called the Washington Bullets won its only NBA title, led by Hall of Fame center Wes Unseld.

👎 LOWEST LOW
A Tough Turn

After four straight 40-plus-win playoff seasons, the Wizards lost their spark in 2008–09, when they won only 19 games.

STUFF

HOME:
Verizon Center

NBA TITLES: 1

ONLY IN WASHINGTON:
The nation's "First Fan," President Barack Obama, has been seen at several Wizards games (he gets good seats!).

STAR SEASONS!

1961
Future Hall of Famer Walt Bellamy was tops in the NBA in field-goal percentage.

1974
Elvin Hayes, "The Big E," led the NBA in rebounding while with a team then known as the Capital Bullets.

1998
Fast-fingered guard Rod Strickland was the NBA's assists leader in the team's first season as Wizards.

WES UNSELD

This Hall of Fame center got off to a good start, as the 1969 NBA Rookie of the Year and MVP. He played 13 season with the franchise, in Baltimore and Washington. Though only 6-7, he was the team's center for most of that time, a fierce and smart rebounding machine. His leadership helped the team win its only NBA title in 1978.

#1

FUNKY FACTS

➜ When he was with the Bullets, Washington big man Gheorghe Muresan wore the number 77. Why? Because he stands 7-feet-7!

➜ In the 2006–07 season, Wizards star Gilbert Arenas donated $100 for every point he scored to local Washington D.C. Schools. He scored more than 2,100 points!

➜ Before 2010 top draft pick John Wall played a game for the Wizards, Washington D.C. mayor Adrian Fenty declared June 25 as "John Wall Day."

➜ Basketball is played indoors, right? But the Wizards had a game cancelled by snow!

SUPERSTAR!

JOSH HOWARD

Howard was an all-around star for the Dallas Mavericks for six-plus seasons before moving to the Wizards in 2010. He'll be a key scoring force for them, as well as a force on the boards.

In February 2010, the Wizards and Denver Nuggets could not fly to Washington D.C. due to a blizzard and their game was postponed!

You Can Look It Up! WASHINGTON'S OFFICIAL WEBSITE: www.nba.com/wizards.com

DENVER NUGGETS

They play their home games a mile above sea level, but the Nuggets are still waiting to end a season miles above the other NBA teams. They have had some exciting, high-scoring teams, however.

GAME 1?
1967

Denver had a team in the first season of the ABA, but it was called the Rockets. They became the Nuggets in 1974 and then joined the NBA in 1976.

MAGIC MOMENT
One Step Away

The Nuggets got *realllly* close to the 2009 NBA Finals, making it to the conference championship, only to lose to the Lakers.

LOWEST LOW
Rocky Mtn. Low

Denver has nearly always had solid seasons, but in 1998, it won only 11 games; it was a few losses shy of an all-time record.

STUFF

HOME:
Pepsi Center

NBA TITLES: 0

ONLY IN DENVER:
Fans look to the dancers and cheerleaders of the "D-Town Squad" to get them psyched up at games.

STAR SEASONS!

1975 The Nuggets set a team record with 65 wins, but were upset in the ABA playoffs by the Indiana Pacers.

1983 In 1983, sweet-shooting forward Alex English became the only Nuggets player to lead the NBA in scoring average.

2008 Denver's big Marcus Camby led the NBA in blocks for the third consecutive year.

The Ultimate Nugget

ALEX ENGLISH

English played in Denver for the last 11 1/2 of his 15 NBA seasons in a Hall of Fame career. He's the Nuggets all-time leader in many key categories: points, assists, steal, and games. An eight-time All-Star, he also led the NBA in field goals three times, mostly thanks to a smooth outside shot and a great ability to glide into the lane.

FUNKY FACTS

→ The Nuggets got their name from gold nuggets that were found in the mountains of Colorado.

→ The Nuggets made the playoffs in each of the nine seasons they played in the ABA . . . but they never won a title!

→ Even though the Nuggets were one of the NBA's top-scoring teams in the 1990-91 season, they had the league's worst record. Local sportswriters started calling them the "Enver" Nuggets, because they had no D!

→ Talk about Rocky Mountain Heights: Huge center Dikembe Mutumbo (a 7-2 native of Congo) led the NBA in blocked

SUPERSTAR! CHAUNCEY BILLUPS

One of the NBA's best free-throw shooters, Billups gives the Nuggets veteran leadership, as well as a deadly three-point shooter. He's back home, too: he played at the University of Colorado.

shots for three straight seasons (1994–96).

→ The Nuggets' mascot, a mountain lion named Rocky, once successfully made his famous backward halfcourt shot in nine consecutive games!

You Can Look It Up! DENVER'S OFFICIAL WEBSITE: www.nba.com/nuggets.com

MINNESOTA
TIMBERWOLVES

Basketball fans in Minnesota have a lot to look back on: The great Minneapolis Lakers teams of the 1950s and the great play of former T-Wolves star Kevin Garnett. With K-G gone, will the T-Wolves howl in the future?

GAME 1?
1989

Minnesota used to be home to the Lakers, but they took their Minny-inspired name and moved to L.A. Twenty-nine years later, the NBA awarded a new team to the state.

MAGIC MOMENT
Wolves Howl!

The T-Wolves had their best season in 2003–04, winning a team-record and Western Conference-best 58 games.

LOWEST LOW
Wolves Woes!

Minnesota had trouble in its early years, posting eight straight losing seasons. The low point was 67 losses in 1991–92.

STUFF

HOME:
Target Center

NBA TITLES: 0

ONLY IN MINNEAPOLIS:
A dance group of kids called the Beat Squad performs each month at Timberwolves games.

STAR SEASONS!

1993
Bringing his championship history from Boston, Kevin McHale became the general manager in Minnesota.

2004
Kevin Garnett led the NBA in rebounding for the first of four straight seasons.

2005
Fred Hoiberg was the most accurate three-point shooter in the NBA, making 48.3 percent of his shots "from downtown."

The Ultimate Timberwolf
KEVIN GARNETT

He's a Boston Celtic now, of course, but his 12 years with the T-Wolves put the team on the map. He led the NBA in rebounding each season from 2004–07, while also pouring in points in buckets. His athletic skills combined with his long arms and 7-0 frame to make him one of the game's best.

#1

FUNKY FACTS

➜ Timberwolves beat out Polars in a naming contest in 1986. The team's home state is the only one in the lower 48 with packs of such animals.

➜ Sharp-shooting Wally Szczerbiak played his first six-and-a-half seasons with the Wolves. How do you say his amazing name? ZER-bee-ack!

➜ Szczerbiak (2002), Sam Casell (2004), and Tom Gugliotta (1997) are the only Timberwolves not named Kevin Garnett to be named to an NBA All-Star Game.

➜ In 1993, the T-Wolves' Michael Williams set an NBA record by making 97 straight free throws.

SUPERSTAR!
JONNY FLYNN

Talented and young, Flynn figures to lead the T-Wolves backcourt for years to come. A star at Syracuse, he moved right into the starting lineup in 2009–10, starting 81 games.

➜ The Target Center has a green roof in more ways than one! The rooftop is a giant garden where numerous plants such as strawberries are grown.

You Can Look It Up! MINNESOTA'S OFFICIAL WEBSITE: www.nba.com/timberwolves.

OKLAHOMA CITY
THUNDER

They play in America's heartland today and boast one of the best young players in the game in Kevin Durant. But this franchise's glory days came in the many years they played in Seattle as the Supersonics.

GAME 1?
1967

The franchise began in Seattle in 1967, joining the NBA instead of the new ABA. Though popular in Seattle, the team moved to Oklahoma City in 2008.

👍 MAGIC MOMENT
Super in Seattle

A team of solid pros, not a superstar among them, put together the first NBA championship in Seattle history in 1979.

👎 LOWEST LOW
Sad Ending

The Supersonics final season in Seattle was tough. They left behind sad fans and a team-record 62 losses in 2007–08.

STUFF

HOME:
Ford Center

NBA TITLES: 1

ONLY IN OKLAHOMA:
You can't dress up as thunder, so the team's mascot is Rumble, who is a giant, slam-dunking bison.

STAR SEASONS!

1970 Lenny Wilkens led the NBA in assists this season. He later became the NBA's all-time winningest coach

1994 Guard Nate McMillan led the NBA in steals, averaging nearly three per game.

2010 Superstar young player Kevin Durant became the first player in franchise history to lead the NBA in scoring.

GARY PAYTON

We're going back in history to find this star (and the Thunder are only two years old), so he's the Ultimate Sonic. Payton brought a great shooting touch and superior passing skills, along with a fierce competitive nature. He played in Seattle for 12 seasons, before ending his NBA career with four teams.

#1

FUNKY FACTS

→ The team's first name, Supersonics, came from an airplane that was built near Seattle by Boeing. Thunder was the winner in a fan contest after the team moved to Oklahoma City.

→ Former Sonics great Xavier "The X-Man" McDaniel used to shave both his head and his eyebrows to look scarier to opponents.

→ The Thunder's mascot, Rumble the Bison, won the NBA Mascot of the Year Award just six months after he made his debut.

→ Dale Ellis holds the record for minutes played in a single

SUPERSTAR! KEVIN DURANT

The NBA scoring champion in 2009–10 with an average of 30.1 points per game, Durant is one of the best young players in the NBA. His long arms and leaping ability make him a scoring star.

game. He scored 53 points in 69 minutes (out of a possible 73) in the Sonics' 155–154 five-overtime loss to the Bucks in 1989.

You Can Look It Up! OKLAHOMA CITY'S OFFICIAL WEBSITE: www.nba.com/thunder.com

PORTLAND
TRAIL BLAZERS

Portland hoops fans have seen a lot of great teams, including a streak of 21 straight playoff berths (1983–2003), but haven't tasted the ultimate victory since 1977. A resurgent squad has high hopes for the future, though.

GAME 1?
1970

The state of Oregon got its first-ever pro sports team when the Trail Blazers started as an NBA expansion team. The name came from Oregon's pioneer past.

MAGIC MOMENT
The Champs!

Led by big men Bill Walton and Maurice Lucas, Portland won its only NBA championship in 1977, beating the Philadelphia 76ers.

LOWEST LOW
Big Upset

The Trail Blazers had the best record in the NBA in 1991, but they stumbled in the Western Conference Finals and lost.

STUFF

HOME:
Rose Garden

NBA TITLES: 1

ONLY IN PORTLAND:
The Rose Garden can be changed into a regular theater when a special "theatrical cloud" lowers from the roof!

STAR SEASONS!

1977 Former UCLA superstar Bill Walton led the NBA in rebounding and blocked shots.

1991 Center Buck Williams led the NBA in field-goal percentage, helping the Blazers win a team-record 63 games.

2010 Portland's star guard Brandon Roy was named to the All-NBA second team for the second time in his career.

The Ultimate Trail Blazer

CLYDE DREXLER

Clyde "The Glide" showed off his amazing aerial skills in 11 1/2 seasons in Portland. He remains the team's all-time leader in points, steals, assists, and rebounds. A 10-time All-Star, Drexler was the Blazers leader on and off the court, helping them reach the playoffs every season he played with the team.

FUNKY FACTS

➔ In 1974, the Blazers played host to President Gerald Ford at the Memorial Coliseum. He was the first president to attend an NBA game. He watched Portland beat the Buffalo Braves 113-106.

➔ Bad move: In the 1984 NBA Draft, the Blazers had the second pick. They chose injury-prone center Sam Bowie over some guy named Michael Jordan.

➔ "Blazermania!" Beginning in April 1977, and lasting until 1995, the Blazers sold out the most consecutive games in pro sports history, packing their home arena a whopping 814 games in a row!

SUPERSTAR! BRANDON ROY

Brandon got off to a fast start, winning the 2007 NBA Rookie of the Year award; he's been an All-Star three times since. He's a key scorer for Portland, as well as running the offense as the point guard!

➔ Until 2011, the Blazers are the only major pro sports team in Oregon. They'll be joined that year by the new Portland Timbers of Major League Soccer.

You Can Look It Up! PORTLAND'S OFFICIAL WEBSITE: www.nba.com/blazers.com

UTAH JAZZ

Their name comes from far away, but since moving to Salt Lake City, this team has become a big part of Utah. Thanks to a famous twosome (see Ultimate Jazz), the club enjoyed a long run of success.

GAME 1?
1974

This team began as an NBA expansion team in New Orleans, so the name comes from the music that fills that city. They kept the name even when the team moved to Utah in 1970.

MAGIC MOMENT
One Step Away

The Jazz set a franchise record with 64 wins and won their first Western Conference title. But they lost to Chicago in the Finals.

LOWEST LOW
Not that Bad

In 1979–80, the Jazz's first year in Utah, fans must have wondered what all the fuss was: The team won only 24 games!

STUFF

HOME:
EnergySolutions Arena

NBA TITLES: 0

ONLY IN UTAH:
Make sure and check out the statues of Ultimate Jazz players John Stockton and Karl Malone outside the arena.

STAR SEASONS!

1984 Adrian Dantley led the NBA in scoring with a 30.6 points per game average; he was the only Utah player to do that.

1985 Mark Eaton had an advantage as he led the NBA in blocked shots for the first of four times: He was 7-5!

2000 Utah's Jeff Hornacek led the league, making 95 percent of his free throws.

The Ultimate Jazz
MALONE/ STOCKTON

It just wouldn't be fair to separate these two Hall of Fame players. Without guard John Stockton's amazing passing (he led the NBA nine straight years in assists), power forward Karl Malone would not have ended up second all-time in the NBA in scoring. They played together in Utah for 18 seasons (1985–2003).

#1

FUNKY FACTS

➜ Talk about loyalty: John Stockton set NBA records for most seasons with one team (19), most games with one team (1,504), and most consecutive games played with one team (he missed only 22 games in his career). He's also the NBA's all-time leader in steals AND assists!

➜ Talk about a comeback! In a 1997 game, the Jazz trailed by 36 points early in the third quarter . . . but came back to win! Their 107–103 win over the Nuggets was the biggest point deficit ever overcome in an NBA game.

➜ Karl Malone was known as "The Mailman," because he always delivered!

SUPERSTAR!
DERON WILLIAMS

No one can replace John Stockton, but Williams is sure giving it a good try. He has been in the top three in the NBA in assists in each of his four NBA seasons, averaging at least 10 per game from 2008–10.

➜ In Game 3 of the 1998 NBA Finals, the Jazz set a rotten record. They scored the fewest points ever in a finals game, losing 96–54.

You Can Look It Up! UTAH'S OFFICIAL WEBSITE: www.nba.com/jazz.com

3RD QUARTER

Hoops is more than just scoring points, of course. You've got to score them with style! The slam dunk is the home run of basketball, intimidating opponents and making reputations. In this chapter, meet the greatest dunkers ever, the men who defy gravity and amaze fans. Also, read about the best passers, rebounders, thieves, and blockers ever. Told you there was more than just scoring!

Three-time NBA dunk champion Nate Robinson shows off.

THE WORLD OF HOOPS

Since the sport began in a small gym in Massachusetts, basketball has spread around the world. It is played in more countries than any other sport except soccer (and some people say it's actually played *more* widely than "futbol"). There are 213 countries in the International Basketball Federation. The top players mostly still head to the NBA, however. In 1982, only six NBA players were born outside the United States . . . in 2010, that number had leaped to 83. Here are the countries represented on NBA rosters to start the 2009–10 season, including how many are from each country.

COUNTRY	NO. OF NBA PLAYERS	COUNTRY	NO. OF NBA PLAYERS
Argentina	5	Georgia	1
Australia	4	Great Britain	3
Belgium	1	Iran	1
Brazil	3	Israel	1
Cameroon	1	Italy	3
Canada	4	Latvia	1
China	2	Lithuania	2
Congo	1	Mexico	1
Croatia	1	Netherlands	2
Dominican Rep.	2	New Zealand	1
France	10	Poland	1

COUNTRY	NO. OF NBA PLAYERS
Puerto Rico*	2
Russia	1
Senegal	1
Serbia	6
Slovenia	5
Spain	5
St. Vincent & Grenadines	1
Sweden	1
Switzerland	1
Tanzania	1
Turkey	3
Ukraine	2
US Virgin Islands*	2

*Yes, we know; these are U.S. territories. But the NBA lists players from there as "international."

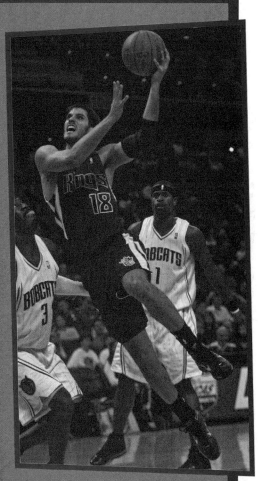

Omri Casspi of Sacramento . . . and Israel!

THE FIRST OUT-OF-TOWNERS

Hank Biasatti was born in Italy and grew up in Canada. In 1946, he played for the Toronto Huskies in the first BAA game. That makes him the first NBA player born outside North America. (Other Canadians played in those early seasons, too.) Bulgaria's Georgi Glouchkov was the first player from Eastern Europe; he joined the Suns in 1985. The first international MVP was Hakeem Olajuwon (1994) of the Rockets and Nigeria. In 2002, Yao Ming became the first foreign player chosen No. 1 overall in the draft.

GREATEST DUNKERS

This is one of those things that can't be nailed down with stats and scores. You can't know for sure who is the greatest slam-dunk artist of all time . . . not for certain. However, there are some players whose creative, high-flying, gravity-defying, sky-walking, ball-slamming feats have them soaring above the crowd. Here's a rundown on our all-time favorites in bringing the hammer.

◀◀◀ Michael Jordan
He was athletic, creative, and clutch. The best all-around player ever, "Air Jordan" certainly included dunking on his list of skills. He once took off from the free-throw line during a dunk contest!

Dominique Wilkins
Long and lean, "The Human Highlight Film" earned his nickname with windmill dunks and high-flying leaps. Wilkins could elevate higher than almost anyone, and his body control was amazing.

Julius Erving
The man known as "Dr. J" revolutionized the dunk. He was the first pro athlete to make stylish, powerful, and defense-embarrassing dunks a big part of his game. He brought ABA style into the NBA and changed the game.

Vince Carter
While playing with Toronto, he was known as "Air Canada" for his soaring skills. His signature dunk was a gymnastic between-the-legs slam that defied gravity.

Jason Richardson
Not a great all-around scorer, he was a dunk specialist who won the Slam Dunk Contest twice with sheer power. Baskets tried to hide when they saw him flying in for another thunder dunk!

Little Big Man

No story of great dunkers can leave out Spud Webb. Standing only 5 feet, 7 inches, Webb had amazing springs. In 1986, he won the NBA Slam Dunk Contest over much taller opponents. Spud soared almost twice his height to take home the trophy!

DUNK TRIVIA

- Beloved Lakers radio man **Chick Hearn** is credited as adding "slam" to "dunk," which had been around since the the 1950s, to create the full name of the shot.

- Slam dunks were illegal in college basketball from 1967–1976. Why? UCLA's **Lew Alcindor**, later called **Kareem Abdul-Jabbar**, was so good at dunking that other teams called it unfair . . . so they passed a rule preventing him from doing it!

A Dawkins Destruction!

- The (partial) name of one of **Darryl Dawkins'** famous monster dunks: The Chocolate-Thunder-Flying, Robinzine*-Crying, Teeth-Shaking, Glass-Breaking, Wham-Bam-I-Am Jam. (***Bill Robinzine** was a player who tried to guard Dawkins.)

- **Georgann Wells** of West Virginia had the first slam dunk in NCAA women's history in a 1984 game. Lisa Leslie of the Los Angeles Sparks smashed home the first dunk in WNBA history in 2002.

- The NBA Slam Dunk Contest has been held since 1984 during the All-Star break. **Nate Robinson** of the New York Knicks became the first player to win the event three times (2006, 2009, 2010).

THANKS FOR THE HELP!

If one thing is true about basketball, it's that it's a team game. Unless you're playing one-on-one in the driveway, you need someone to pass you the ball if you want to score. The person passing gets an assist. Here are the all-time most helpful players.

NBA

PLAYER	ASSISTS/GAME
◀ Magic **Johnson**	**11.2**
John **Stockton**	**10.5**
Chris **Paul**	**9.99**
Oscar **Roberton**	**9.5**
Isiah **Thomas**	**9.3**
Jason **Kidd**	**9.2**
Kevin **Johnson**	**9.1**
Deron **Williams**	**9.0**
Norm **Nixon**	**8.3**
Steve **Nash**	**8.3**
Tim **Hardaway**	**8.2**
Kevin **Porter**	**8.1**

Single-Game Records

The all-time NBA record for helpfulness in a game came in 1990, when Scott Skiles of the Orlando Magic dished out 30 assists in their 155–116 win over the Denver Nuggets. The game was played on December 30, so think of all those passes as belated Christmas presents! Three players tied for the NCAA single-game record with 22.

NCAA assists leader Avery Johnson (left) is now a successful NBA coach.

NCAA

PLAYER, SCHOOL	ASSISTS/GAME
Avery **Johnson,** SOUTHERN	12.0
Sam **Crawford,** NEW MEXICO STATE	8.8
Mark **Wade,** OKLAHOMA/UNLV	8.8
Chris **Corchiani,** N.C. STATE	8.4
Taurence **Chisholm,** DELAWARE	8.0
Van **Usher,** TENNESSEE TECH	8.0
Anthony **Manuel,** BRADLEY	7.9
Chico **Fletcher,** ARKANSAS STATE	7.8
Gary **Payton,** OREGON STATE	7.8
Orlando **Smart,** SAN FRANCISCO	7.8

HITTING THE BOARDS

NBA

PLAYER	REBOUNDS/GAME
Wilt **Chamberlain**	22.9
Bill **Russell**	22.5
Bob **Pettit**	16.2
Jerry **Lucas**	15.6
Nate **Thurmond**	15.0
Wes **Unseld**	14.0
Walt **Bellamy**	13.7
Dave **Cowens**	13.6
Elgin **Baylor**	13.6
George **Mikan**	13.4
Dennis **Rodman**	13.1
Willis **Reed**	12.9

WILT THE STILT

In a 1960 game against the Celtics, Wilt Chamberlain of the Philadephia Warriors snagged a stunning 55 rebounds to set what is certainly an almost unbreakable record.

Russell vs. Chamberlain

Hitting boards does not mean that all basketball players are karate experts whacking plywood. The "boards," of course, is slang for the backboard. It's the place rebounders go to snag missed shots. Grabbing rebounds takes size, skill, practice, and guts. Here are the best rebounders in pro and college history.

NCAA

PLAYER, SCHOOL	REBOUNDS/GAME
Artis **Gilmore**, JACKSONVILLE	22.7
Charlie **Slack**, MARSHALL	21.8
Paul **Silas**, CREIGHTON	21.6
Leroy **Wright**, PACIFIC	21.5
Art **Quimby**, CONNECTICUT	21.5
Walt **Dukes**, SETON HALL	21.1
Bill **Russell**, SAN FRANCISCO	20.3
Kermit **Washington**, AMERICAN	20.2
Julius **Erving**, MASSACHUSETTS	20.2
Joe **Holup**, GEORGE WASHINGTON	19.5
Elgin **Baylor**, COLL. OF IDAHO/SEATTLE	19.5
Dave **DeBusschere**, DETROIT	19.4

ARTIS

If you were looking for Artis Gilmore during his 17-year pro career, you would probably find him near the basket. He led the ABA in rebounding four times (and blocks three times) while with the Kentucky Colonels, winning the league MVP trophy in 1972. Then after he moved to the Chicago Bulls in the NBA, he led that league in field-goal percentage. You usually win that category by making a lot of close-range shots; for Gilmore, many of those came after offensive rebounds.

THIEF!

Quick hands and the daring of a burglar: That's that it takes to make a steal in a basketball game. A steal can turn the momentum of a game in an instant . . . and it can make an opponent look baaaad! Here are the best ball-stealers ever.

NBA

PLAYER	STEALS/GAME
Alvin **ROBERTSON**	2.71
Micheal Ray **RICHARDSON**	2.63
Jerry **WEST**	2.61
Michael **JORDAN**	2.35
Mookie **BLAYLOCK**	2.33
Fat **LEVER**	2.22
Slick **WATTS**	2.20

NCAA

PLAYER, SCHOOL	STEALS/GAME
Mookie **BLAYLOCK**, OKLAHOMA	3.80
Ronn **McMAHON**, EAST. WASHINGTON	3.52
Desmond **CAMBRIDGE**, ALABAMA A&M	3.40
Eric **MURDOCK**, PROVIDENCE	3.21
Van **USHER**, TENNESSEE TECH	3.18
John **LINEHAN**, PROVIDENCE	3.16
Pepe **SANCHEZ**, TEMPLE	3.15

BLOCKED!

Being really tall helps a player become good at blocking shots. But it also takes perfect timing and the courage to go up in the air against an athletic shooter. Blocks, like steals, are also a weapon in the mental game of hoops. Reject a shooter and next time, he might think twice about going up against you! Here are the all-time best.

NBA

PLAYER	BLOCKS/GAME
Mark **EATON**	3.50
Manute **BOL**	3.34
Hakeem **OLAJUWON**	3.09
David **ROBINSON**	2.99
Elmore **SMITH**	2.90
Alonzo **MOURNING**	2.81
Dikembe **MUTOMBO**	2.75

NCAA

PLAYER, SCHOOL	BLOCKS/GAME
Keith **CLOSS**, CENTRAL CONN. ST.	5.87
Adonal **FOYLE**, COLGATE	5.66
David **ROBINSON**, NAVY	5.24
Mickell **GLADNESS**, ALABAMA A&M	4.66
Wojciech **MYDRA**, LA-MONROE	4.65
Shaquille **O'NEAL**, LSU	4.58
Troy **MURPHY**, NOTRE DAME	4.52

RECORDS

The single-game record for most blocks in an NBA game is 17, set by Elmore Smith in 1973. Mickell Gladness rejected 16 shots in a 2007 game to set the NCAA record.

DALLAS
MAVERICKS

With the NBA's most famous owner in Internet mogul Mark Cuban, the Mavericks' great play sometimes gets lost in the shuffle. However, they have been one of the league's best teams for the past decade.

GAME 1?
1980

After the ABA's Dallas team moved to San Antonio, Big D was without a pro hoops team until they got an expansion team. The name comes from an old cowboy word.

MAGIC MOMENT
Just Shy

In 2006, the Mavericks won their first Western Conference championship, but then lost in the NBA Finals to Miami.

LOWEST LOW
Not Quite Great

The 2007 Mavs won a team-record 67 games and looked like champions. But they were upset in the playoffs by Golden State.

STUFF

HOME:
American Airlines Center

NBA TITLES: 0

ONLY IN DALLAS:
Mavs owner Mark Cuban often sits near courtside, cheering for his team . . . and yelling at refs!

STAR SEASONS!

1984 Forward Mark Aguirre led the NBA in field goals in the team's first winning season.

2002 Future NBA MVP (with Phoenix) Steve Nash earned the first of two All-Star selections while with Dallas.

2004 Antawn Jamison was named the NBA Sixth Man of the Year for his contributions to the team off the bench.

The Ultimate Maverick

DIRK NOWITZKI

We like to have different players for Ultimate and Superstar, but in the case of Nowitzki, he's got to be both. He's the Mavericks' all-time leader in points, rebounds, and games. He's even second in blocks and steals! Dirk's a nine-time All-Star and was the 2007 NBA MVP, the first player from Europe (he's German) to win that honor.

FUNKY FACTS

➔ The Mavericks have two mascots—a blue horse named "Champ" and a high-flying daredevil named "Mavs Man" whose skin looks like the surface of a basketball!

➔ Mavericks guard Jason Terry plays every game with five pairs of socks on because he says it's more comfortable!

➔ The Mavericks' alternate road jerseys—green and blue with "Mavs" on the front, were designed by rapper and fashion mogul Sean "P. Diddy" Combs.

➔ The Mavs ManiAACs are a group of, well . . . beefy guys. They "dance" around and perform at Mavs games. They

SUPERSTAR! DIRK NOWITZKI

Here he is again! Nowitzki is a unique talent, with the size (7-0, 240 pounds) to play a tough inside game, but an outside shooting touch that lets him average nearly 40 percent on three-point shots.

have strange names such as Chunky D, Wonder Bread, and Ice Ike Baby.

You Can Look It Up! DALLAS'S OFFICIAL WEBSITE: www.nba.com/mavericks.com

HOUSTON ROCKETS

Like the spaceships they are named for, the Rockets have blasted to great heights, winning two NBA titles. They also landed back on Earth—their last title was 15 years ago! But they have talent to shoot for the stars again.

GAME 1? 1967

The Rockets first blasted into the NBA in 1967 in San Diego. It was perfect when they moved to Houston in 1976, since that city was the home of NASA and its rockets!

👍 MAGIC MOMENT
1994 Champs!

Led by the great center Hakeem Olajuwon, Houston won its first NBA championship. Then they did it again in 1995.

👎 LOWEST LOW
1983 Chumps!

Just two seasons after making the NBA Finals, the Rockets crashed back to earth, losing a team-record 68 games.

STUFF

HOME:
Toyota Center

NBA TITLES: 2

ONLY IN HOUSTON:
Clutch the Bear, the team's mascot, is famous for flinging large sheet cakes into the face of "enemy fans."

STAR SEASONS!

1979 Moses Malone won the first of his six NBA rebounding titles. He won three with Houston and three with Philly.

1989 Another powerful big man, Hakeem Olajuwon, led the NBA in blocks for the first of three seasons.

2010 The Rockets' Aaron Brooks led the NBA by making 209 three-point shots.

The Ultimate Rocket

HAKEEM OLAJUWON

Born in Nigeria and taken with the first pick of the 1984 NBA Draft, Hakeem "The Dream" is one of best centers ever. A 12-time All-Star and two-time NBA Finals MVP (and 1994 NBA MVP), Olajuwon is the Rockets' all-time leader in points, rebounds, steals, blocked shots, and games. He led them to both of their NBA titles.

#1

FUNKY FACTS

➔ Hall-of-Famer Rick Barry played his final NBA game in 1980, when he was on the Rockets. His sons, Brent and Jon, also played in the NBA and ended their careers with the team.

➔ The Rockets got a new logo in 1995. Thanks to some help from NASA and its astronauts, the new logo was first shown to the public . . . in outer space aboard the Space Shuttle!

➔ On December 9, 2004, Tracy McGrady led a wild Rockets comeback win over the Spurs by scoring 13 points in 33 seconds!

➔ China-born star Yao Ming got to show his teammates

SUPERSTAR! YAO MING

At 7-6, he's the NBA's tallest player. He's a seven-time All-Star and pretty much impossible to shoot over! He is bouncing back in 2010 from a foot injury that made him miss a season.

around his homeland when they played 2010 preseason games against the Nets in China. Not surprisingly, the team drew crowds of Yao-loving fans.

You Can Look It Up! HOUSTON'S OFFICIAL WEBSITE: www.nba.com/rockets.com

MEMPHIS GRIZZLIES

Well, their mascot is cool! The Grizzlies have struggled to find success in both of their homes: Canada and Tennessee. In 15 seasons, they have only three winning records. But hope springs eternal in the South!

GAME 1?
1995

One of the league's several 1990s expansion teams, the Grizzlies started in Vancouver as Canada's second modern NBA team. They moved to Memphis in 2001.

MAGIC MOMENT
Finally, a Winner!

In their ninth NBA sesaon, the 2004 Grizzlies posted their first winning record and made the playoffs for the first time.

LOWEST LOW
8 for '99

With the season cut short due to labor troubles, the Grizzlies were happy; they won only eight games—it could have been worse!

STUFF

HOME:
FedEx Forum

NBA TITLES: 0

ONLY IN MEMPHIS:
The Grizzlies mascot is imported. "Grizz" moved to Tennessee from Canada with the team.

STAR SEASONS!

1998 Sharif Adbur-Rahim set the team record for scoring by pouring in 1,829 points.

2006 Forward Pau Gasol earned the first All-Star game spot by a Memphis Grizzly.

2010 Zach Randolph led the NBA in offensive rebounds. Those are rebounds made after a teammate misses a shot (defensive boards come when an opponent misses).

The Ultimate Grizzly
PAU GASOL

He's a Lakers star today, but Spain's Pau Gasol was the heart of the Grizzlies for six-and-a-half seasons (2001–08). He led them to all three of their playoff appearances, and he remains the team's all-time leader in games, points, and rebounds. One of the players Memphis got when Pau was traded to the Lakers was his brother Marc!

FUNKY FACTS

➜ When the Grizzlies were established in 1995, they became the first NBA team to have a Web site.

➜ The Grizzlies' first-ever draft pick was Bryant "Big Country" Reeves. The Arkansas native lived up to his nickname. Reeves was 7 feet tall and weighed 275 pounds.

➜ Grizzlies center Hamed Haddadi became the first player in NBA history from the country of Iran when he debuted with the team in 2008.

➜ When Grizzlies star Rudy Gay was selected to participate in the 2008 Slam Dunk Contest, he asked fans to post videos of cool-looking dunks on YouTube so that he could try some of them in the contest. He tried, but did not advance into the second round.

SUPERSTAR! ZACH RANDOLPH

A powerful forward and rebounder, Randolph earned an All-Star selection in his first year with the Grizzlies in 2010. He had played for the Trail Blazers, Knicks, and Clippers.

You Can Look It Up! MEMPHIS'S OFFICIAL WEBSITE: www.nba.com/grizzlies.com

NEW ORLEANS
HORNETS

Though the Hornets are still one of the NBA's newer teams, with seven playoff berths in the past decade, they've certainly made their mark. Their loyalty to their newest home in Louisiana also makes them winners!

GAME 1?
1988

The Hornets first built their hive in Charlotte but buzzed off to New Orleans in 2002. They played for a year in Oklahoma (see Funky Facts) but have settled in New Orleans to stay.

MAGIC MOMENT
2008 Was Great

A division championship and a spot in the conference semifinals made this the best season in the team's short history.

LOWEST LOW
2005 Was Jive

The Hornets had made the playoffs for five straight seasons before falling out of the race by winning only 18 games this year.

STUFF

HOME:
New Orleans Arena

NBA TITLES: 0

ONLY IN NEW ORLEANS:
Hornets' mascot Hugo has two other personalities: dunk machine Super Hugo and opponent-bothering Air Hugo.

STAR SEASONS!

1993 After being the second overall pick in the NBA draft, center Alonzo Mourning makes the NBA All-Rookie team.

2008 Peja Stojakovic was the best free-throw shooter in the NBA, making 92.9 percent of his shots from the charity stripe.

2008 Chris Paul led the NBA in steals at 2.17 per game, and assists at 11.6.

The Ultimate Hornet
MUGGSY BOGUES

Forward Dell Curry deserves a mention here as the Hornets' all-time leading scorer, but we'll give this award to talented point guard Muggsy Bogues. At 5-3, he was the shortest player in league history, but played 14 NBA seasons, including nine of his prime years with the Hornets.

FUNKY FACTS

→ When they started play in 1988, the Hornets received a lot of attention when they chose teal as their color. The NHL's San Jose Sharks, NFL's Jacksonville Jaguars, MLB's Florida Marlins and other pro and amateur clubs soon followed with similar colors. Copycats!

→ Did you know that Lakers' star Kobe Bryant was very, very briefly a Hornet? The Hornets took Bryant with the 13th overall pick in 1996. However, he was immediately traded to Los Angeles for center Vlade Divac.

→ Because of the devastation caused by Hurricane Katrina in New Orleans in 2005, the Hornets played most of their games in Oklahoma City in 2005-06 and 2006-07. They were officially called the New Orleans/Oklahoma City Hornets. The team's popularity there led to the Seattle Supersonics moving to Oklahoma in 2008 and becoming the Thunder.

SUPERSTAR! CHRIS PAUL

Paul is one of the NBA's most talented guards. He has twice led the NBA in assists and steals while making three All-Star Games. He was the 2006 Rookie of the Year.

You Can Look It Up! NEW ORLEANS'S OFFICIAL WEBSITE: www.nba.com/hornets.com

SAN ANTONIO SPURS

With four NBA titles in a nine-year span, the Spurs established themselves as one of the NBA's dynasties, and one of its best all-around teams. Boasting a host of great players, they're sure to "spur" new championships ahead!

GAME 1?
1967

Originally the Dallas Chaparrals of the ABA, the team changed cities and names (to their current ones) in 1973, then changed leagues (to the NBA) in 1976.

 ## MAGIC MOMENT
Title No. 1

Led by the "Twin Towers," David Robinson and Tim Duncan, the Spurs knocked off the Knicks to win their first NBA title in 1999.

LOWEST LOW
Tough Season

The Spurs have had very few losing seasons. Their most recent was a 20–62 campaign way back in 1996–97.

STUFF

HOME:
AT&T Center

NBA TITLES: 4

ONLY IN SAN ANTONIO:
The Spurs' mascot, The Coyote, was signed as a "flea agent" in 1983 and is the NBA's "Most Valuable Varmint."

STAR SEASONS!

1975 Back in the old ABA days, Spurs center Swen Nater led that young league in rebounding.

1978 George "The Iceman" Gervin, one of the best shooters ever, won the first of his four NBA scoring titles with a 27.2 points per game average.

1991 The talented center David Robinson led the NBA in rebounding.

DAVID ROBINSON

With Tim Duncan earning Superstar honors, we'll make his one-time frontcourt partner Robinson the Ultimate Spur. Known as "The Admiral," since he was in the Navy before joining the team full-time, he was a 10-time All-Star, the 1990 Rookie of the Year, a scoring and rebounding champ, and part of two of the Spurs title runs.

#1

FUNKY FACTS

➔ The team was briefly called the Gunslingers after they moved to San Antonio, but it was changed before they played a game!

➔ Two of only four officially recorded quadruple-doubles in NBA history (double digits in four out of five categories of points, rebounds, assists, steals, and blocks) were recorded by Spurs players Alvin Robertson (1986) and David Robinson (1994).

➔ The Spurs played in front of the largest NBA Finals crowd (39,554 in Game 2) in 1999 at the Alamodome.

➔ Talk about a comeback! Sean Elliott was the first NBA player to return and play in a

SUPERSTAR! TIM DUNCAN

A surefire Hall of Famer, Duncan is one of the best all-around players in the league. A two-time NBA MVP and three-time NBA Finals MVP, he's been the centerpiece of the team since he joined the Spurs in 1997.

game after a major organ transplant. After receiving a kidney transplant, he scored his first points in 2000 by dunking over 7-2 center Dikembe Mutumbo.

You Can Look It Up! SAN ANTONIO'S OFFICIAL WEBSITE: www.nba.com/spurs.com

4TH QUARTER

We're all over the court in this chapter. We'll fill you in on the women's game. Then we'll take our best shot at choosing the best ever at all the key positions. Finally, meet some great coaches, see who runs the NBA, and visit the Hall of Fame. Whew!

INSIDE:

The best women in basketball battle it out in the WNBA.

THE
WNBA

Women have been playing basketball since the beginning (page 13), but they didn't get their own big-time U.S. pro league until 1997. The WNBA was formed as a part of the larger NBA. Women's college basketball was improving every year, but the top players went to other countries to play. With the WNBA, women had a top-flight league. Here's a rundown on the 2010 teams, along with the years they started and the championships they've won.

2008
Atlanta Dream

2000
Indiana Fever

2006
Chicago Sky

1997
Los Angeles Sparks
CHAMPIONSHIPS: **2001, 2002**

1999
Connecticut Sun*

1999
Minnesota Lynx

Other WNBA Teams

Some WNBA teams lasted only a few seasons. Here's a rundown if you're ever in a basketball trivia contest. The years show when they played.

Charlotte Sting 1997–2006

Cleveland Rockers 1997–2003

Houston Comets* 1997–2008

Miami Sol 2000–2002

Portland Fire 2000–2002

Sacramento Monarchs** 1997–2008

*WNBA Champs: 1997, 1998, 1999, 2000   **WNBA Champs: 2005

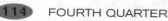

1997
New York Liberty

1997
Phoenix Mercury
CHAMPIONSHIPS: **2007, 2009**

1997
San Antonio Silver Stars**

2000
Seattle Storm
CHAMPIONSHIPS: **2004, 2010**

1998
Tulsa Shock#
CHAMPIONSHIPS:
2003, 2006, 2008

1998
Washington Mystics

*Began as Orlando Miracle and moved to Connecticut in 2003; ** began as Utah Starzz and moved to San Antonio in 2003; # began as Detroit Shock and moved to Tulsa in 2009

Seattle star Sue Bird celebrates the Storm's 2010 WNBA title.

Another Way to Pro

The WNBA was not the first try at a women's pro league, just the most successful. From 1978–1981, the Women's Basketball League played with eight teams. They featured stars such as Nancy Lieberman and Ann Meyers. Other women's leagues lasted even less time.

WNBA STARS

Here are some of the top players in the WNBA today:

Tamika Catchings
F, Indiana Fever
Six-time All-Star and three-time defensive player of the year, she's a true power forward.

Katie Douglas
G, Indiana Fever
Three-time All-Star who is super at both ends of the floor.

◀ Lauren Jackson
F, Seattle Storm
Australia native, super ball-handler, seven-time All-Star.

Diana Taurasi
G, Phoenix Mercury
Four-time All-Star, 2009 MVP, outstanding all-around player and scorer, helped UConn win three titles.

Special Mention

Here are three former players who deserve mention among the best:

Cynthia Cooper-Dyke She helped the Houston Rockets win four straight WNBA championships and was named the league's MVP in 1999 and 2000.

Lisa Leslie Leslie retired in 2009 as the WNBA's greatest star. A part of the league since from its first season, she helped L.A. win a pair of WNBA titles and she won three MVP awards. She was the first to dunk in a game, and her celebrity helped spread the word about the WNBA.

Sheryl Swoopes She was a three-time MVP who was a big presence inside for the Houston Comets, with whom she won the 2000 championship.

BEFORE
THE WNBA

The WNBA has been home to the best women's players in the world since 1997. But women were hoops stars before then. Here's a quick look at some of the pioneers of big-time women's b-ball.

NANCY LIEBERMAN One of the most famous female players ever, she was a two-time national champion at Old Dominion and was twice named the top female athlete in the nation. She helped the U.S. win a 1976 Olympic silver medal, and later played in two pro leagues. She also played for a men's team in the USBL before coaching in the WNBA.

ANN MEYERS Her all-around talents made her the first four-time All-America ever at UCLA–male or female. She went on to play in the WBL and even had a tryout with the NBA's Pacers.

CHERYL MILLER ▶▶▶

Perhaps the best college player ever, she was a four-time All-America and three-time Naismith Award winner. She also won an Olympic gold medal in 1984 and set a high school record with 105 points in one game in 1982!

LYNETTE WOODARD

After starring for the University of Kansas, where she set an NCAA record for most career points, Woodard became the first woman to play for the Harlem Globetrotters in 1985.

CENTERS
BEST OF ALL-TIME

For most of basketball's first 100 years, the center was ... well, the center of the game. A big man in the middle could dominate the game. Here's a rundown of the best centers of all time.

KAREEM ABDUL-JABBAR **Bucks/Lakers: 1969–1989**
All-time leading scorer in NBA; won six MVP awards and two NBA Finals MVPs; 19-time All-Star; won six NBA championships; inventor of famous, impossible-to-block "Sky Hook" shot; after his career, became an author of nonfiction and history.

BILL RUSSELL
Celtics: 1956–69
Led Boston to an amazing 11 NBA titles; won four NBA MVP awards; as player-coach in 1966, became first African-American to lead major U.S. sports team; considered best defensive center ever; his battles with Wilt Chamberlain were among the fiercest head-to-head rivalries in sports. Wilt won most, but Russell won the titles.

Bill Russell with coach Red Auerbach

WILT CHAMBERLAIN **Warriors/76ers/Lakers: 1959–73**
An unstoppable force on offense, "Wilt the Stilt" was the only player to average more than 50 points a game in a season; only player to score 100 points in a game; four-time NBA MVP; one of the greatest rebounders ever as well, known as "The Big Dipper."

HAKEEM OLAJUWON **Rockets/Raptors: 1984–2002**
First player named MVP, Finals MVP, and defensive player of the year in same year (1994); powerful rebounder and inside scorer, "Hakeem the Dream" led Rockets to two NBA titles; 12-time All-Star.

TODAY'S BEST

The center is not as big a part of many teams' offenses today. The three-point shot and a quicker passing game has tamed the ability of the "big man" to dominate a game. However, some players of today, with great size and skill, have continued the legacy of Russell, Kareem, and the Stilt.

Tim Duncan

FIRST SEASON: 1997
TEAM: SAN ANTONIO SPURS

Sort of a forward/center, Duncan has not had the national media attention of some other superstars, but NBA fans know how good this guy really is. A regular among rebounding leaders, he is also a defensive force. Duncan has helped the Spurs win three NBA titles, winning the NBA Finals MVP each time. A two-time NBA MVP, Duncan is also the only player ever to be named All-NBA and All-Defensive Team in each of his first 12 seasons.

▲

Shaquille O'Neal

FIRST SEASON: 1992
TEAMS: MAGIC, LAKERS, HEAT, SUNS, CAVALIERS, CELTICS

A three-time NBA champion with the Lakers, "Shaq Daddy" dominated games for a decade. He led the Lakers to three straight NBA titles (2000–2002) and won a fourth with the Miami Heat in 2004. O'Neal is a three-time NBA MVP and a two-time scoring champion; he has also won three All-Star Game MVPs. His outsized personality matches his playing skills, making him one of the most famous and popular players ever.

Dwight Howard

FIRST SEASON: 2004
TEAM: ORLANDO MAGIC

Known as Superman, Howard is probably the best overall big man in the NBA today. He almost singlehandedly carried the Magic to the 2009 NBA Finals. A three-time defensive player of the year, in 2010 Howard became the first player to lead the NBA in rebounding, blocked shots and field goal percentage in the same season.

FORWARDS
BEST OF ALL-TIME

ELGIN BAYLOR Lakers: 1958–72
Baylor was a high-scoring, highlight-reel player for some great Lakers teams. A 10-time All-NBA player, he was making moves and shots years before they were parts of many athletic players' games.

KARL MALONE Jazz: 1985–2004
Known as "The Mailman," Malone delivered the second-most points in NBA history during his long career. Most of his points came from the inside, as he used his strength and size to battle toward the basket.

◀◀◀LARRY BIRD Celtics: 1979–92
Considered one of the best all-around players ever, Bird excelled at passing and had a deadly outside shot (he won the first three NBA Three-Point Shot Contests), as well as near-perfection from the free-throw line. One of the fiercest competitors ever, he led the Celtics to three NBA titles in the 1980s.

DR. J Virginia Squires/NY Nets: 1971–1976 (ABA); 76ers: 1976–1987
Julius Erving was called "Dr. J" because of how well he operated on the court. His dunking ability revolutionized the game and created enormous interest in a high-flying type of basketball. A three-time ABA MVP, the Doctor also helped the 76ers win the 1983 NBA title.

RICK BARRY Oakland, Washington, Nets (ABA): 1968–1972; Warriors/Rockets (NBA): 1965–67, 1972–1980
Famous for shooting free throws underhand (he was a seven-time league leader and he's fifth all-time in percentage), Barry could score from anywhere. He is the only player to lead the NCAA, ABA, and NBA in scoring. He helped the Warriors win their only title in 1975.

TODAY'S BEST

Kevin Durant

FIRST SEASON: 2007

TEAM: SONICS/THUNDER

This up-and-coming star emerged in 2010. Durant became the youngest-ever scoring champ in, scoring 30.1 points per game.

LeBron James

FIRST SEASON: 2003

TEAMS: CAVALIERS, HEAT

A two-time MVP and former scoring champion, "The King" is one of the best all-around players in the game today. He pulled the Cavs into the league elite by himself, but stunned Cleveland fans in 2010 by moving to the

Miami Heat. Few players combine his outside scoring touch with such a powerful inside game.

Pau Gasol

FIRST SEASON: 2001

TEAMS: GRIZZLIES, LAKERS

Born in Spain, Gasol proved to be the key piece of the puzzle that helped the L.A. Lakers win a pair of NBA titles (2009, 2010). Though he's seven feet tall, he moves like a smaller player and has a great outside touch.

Kevin Garnett

FIRST SEASON: 1995

TEAMS: TIMBERWOLVES, CELTICS

After a long stint with Minnesota, where he played in 10 All-Star Games and built a reputation for toughness in the paint, "KG" moved to Boston and helped the Celtics win the 2008 NBA title). Garnett jumped right to the NBA in 1995 without going to college.

◀Dirk Nowitzki

FIRST SEASON: 1998

TEAM: MAVERICKS

This German native has spent his entire career as the anchor of the Mavs team. Like many European big men, he can shoot very well from outside. That makes him tough to defend, since he can also go the basket like a guard.

GUARDS
BEST OF ALL-TIME

Guards run the show on the basketball court. They're expected to do just about everything: make entry passes, hit jump shots, penetrate for layups, lead fast breaks, and defend opposing guards. It's a busy job that combines physical skills with basketball smarts. Here are quick looks at the best from yesterday and today.

OSCAR ROBERTSON
Royals/Bucks: 1960–74

How multi-talented was the "Big O"? He averaged a triple-double for an entire season! That means he averaged 10 or more points, assists, and rebounds every game. Few players before or since have been as good as so many parts of the game as Robertson was.

JERRY WEST   Lakers: 1960–74

After a fantastic college career, West carried his smooth game to the NBA with the Lakers. His ball-control skills were so good that his form was actually used as the basis for the NBA logo. He was such a dependable shooter that his nickname was "Mr. Clutch." As an executive, he helped the Lakers win six titles and later helped run the Grizzlies.

EARVIN "MAGIC" JOHNSON   Lakers: 1979–91, 1995–96

The first "big" point guard (6-8), Magic led the Lakers' "Showtime" offense to three NBA titles. His no-look passes, his clutch scoring, and his ever-present smile made him one of the most popular players of all time. His retirement due to HIV infection (the virus that causes AIDS) also made him a courageous leader for people with the disease. He's now a businessman and a part-owner of the Lakers.

MICHAEL JORDAN   Bulls/Wizards: 1984–1998, 2001–03

Most experts call Jordan the best player of all time at any position. A 10-time NBA scoring champion, a six-time NBA Finals MVP, a six-time NBA champ, and five-time NBA MVP, "Air Jordan" rocketed to stardom as a high-flying dunk machine. He grew over time into a complete player as fierce on D as he was on offense. He was always clutch and later became a fiery leader, too. Today, Jordan is an owner of the Charlotte Bobcats.

TODAY'S BEST

Today's guards fall into two categories: point guards with passing skills and shooting guards who light up the scoreboard. Both are vital to a team's success. Here are the best of today's backcourt players.

Kobe Bryant ▶

FIRST SEASON: 1996
TEAM: LAKERS

The best all-around player in today's NBA, Bryant has led the Lakers to five NBA titles (through 2010) and won two NBA Finals MVP awards (he's also a three-time All-Star Game MVP!). He has led the NBA in scoring twice and regularly makes shots that defy description. His 81-point game in 2006 was second-highest ever.

Joe Johnson

FIRST SEASON: 2003
TEAM: CELTICS/SUNS/HAWKS

How important is Johnson to the Hawks? They made him their highest-paid player in 2010. He not only dishes assists, but he's averaged at least 20 points a game five times.

Deron Williams

FIRST SEASON: 2005
TEAM: JAZZ

Williams has very ably filled the giant sneaker prints left by Hall of Fame point guard John Stockton in Utah. Williams's quick passing has helped him reach double digits in assists average four times.

Steve Nash

FIRST SEASON: 1996
TEAM: SUNS/MAVERICKS

Nash is probably the best pure passing guard in the league. His ability to find open teammates, as well as hit clutch shots, helped him become the first Canadian-born player to win the MVP in 2005.

Dwyane Wade

FIRST SEASON: 2003
TEAM: HEAT

In 2006, only his third season, DWade led the Heat to their only NBA championship. Since then, he has cemented his rep as one of the NBA's most feared scoring machines.

CLIPBOARD KINGS

Why are there so many timeouts late in basketball games? So coaches can earn their money. Basketball coaches have to combine great ideas about the game with an ability to mold a dozen individual athletes into a solid team. The best coaches are able to take the best players . . . and make them better. Here's a quick look at some memorable coaches from the pros and college.

◄◄◄ **RED AUERBACH** Auerbach (pronounced OW-er-back) was a part of the Celtics for an amazing 57 years, including 16 as head coach. He was later the general manager and president. His teams won nine NBA titles, after each of which he lit his famous "victory cigar."

GENO AURIEMMA Auriemma has led the University of Connecticut women's team to six NCAA titles. His teams have posted three undefeated seasons, including back-to-back in 2009 and 2010. Entering 2010-11, UConn was on a 78-game win streak.

PHIL JACKSON With the Bulls, Jackson blended the talents of Michael Jordan with others to win six titles. Moving to the Lakers, he guided Kobe and Shaq and many others to five more crowns. Jackson's 11 titles are the most in NBA history.

ADOLPH RUPP Leading the University of Kentucky from 1930–72, Rupp won 876 games, third-most all-time. His teams won four NCAA championships.

DEAN SMITH The longtime coach of the University of North Carolina, Smith is second all-time with 879 victories. His Tar Heels teams won a pair of NCAA titles, he guided the 1976 U.S. Olympic team, and was a four-time coach of the year.

JOHN WOODEN With a probably-unbreakable record of 10 NCAA titles, including seven in a row (1967–73), Wooden is the greatest college coach ever. His teams once won a record 88 games in a row. His "Pyramid of Success," ideas on how to live a good, positive life, are used in schools around the country.

NBA
COMMISSIONERS

The NBA is run by the commissioner, who is elected by the owners and signed to a contract. Since the leagues that became the NBA were founded in 1946, there have been only four NBA commissioners. They each had their own skills, but each helped the league grow. The current commissioner, David Stern, is regarded as one of the most powerful men in world sports.

DAVID STERN, 1984–▶▶▶

Has presided over the NBA's greatest growth, adding teams in Canada . . . expanded use of NBA.com and international TV . . . has taken NBA to dozens of countries around the world . . . oversaw numerous labor deals to keep players and owners happy.

LAWRENCE O'BRIEN,

1975–1984 Former adviser to Pres. John Kennedy . . . oversaw merger with ABA in late 1970s . . . helped forge first contract with players' union . . . league championship trophy is named for O'Brien.

WALTER KENNEDY, 1963–1975 Former

league publicity director and mayor in Connecticut . . . league doubled in size under his leadership . . . league added teams on both coasts and reached new highs in attendance.

MAURICE PODOLOFF, 1946–1963 Helped

form the BAA . . . forged merger with the NBL that led to today's NBA . . . lawyer who also oversaw creation of the 24-second clock, the biggest change to basketball rules since Naismith.

THE
HALL OF FAME

Every sport needs a place to honor its greatest contributors. In 1959, the Naismith Memorial Basketball Hall of Fame was founded to do just that. The Hall was built, naturally, in Springfield, Massachusetts . . . the home of the very first basketball game in 1891. Each year, the Hall adds new members, including players, coaches, referees, international stars, and others. Unlike most other Halls of Fame, the Naismith also includes whole teams, such as the 1992 Olympic Dream Team.

KINDS OF MEMBERS

Here's how the members of the Hall of Fame break down into categories:

PLAYERS:	145*
COACHES:	83
TEAMS:	8
REFEREES:	13
CONTRIBUTORS:	57**

*Thirteen of those players are women, the most in any of the big pro sports halls of fame.

**Including commissioners, team owners, broadcasters, international leaders, etc.

FIRST CLASS!

Here's a quick rundown of the people and teams who were the first to be inducted into the Basketball Hall of Fame in 1959:

Forrest C. "Phog" Allen: longtime Kansas coach

Henry Clifford Carlson: longtime Pittsburgh coach

First Team: Naismith's first squad of players

Luther H. Gulick: YMCA leader who helped Naismith

Edward J. "Ed" Hickox: coach who helped found Hall of Fame

Charles D. "Chuck" Hyatt: college and AAU star

Angelo "Hank" Luisetti: Stanford star shooter

Walter E. Meanwell: longtime Wisconsin coach

George Mikan: helped his teams win seven NBA titles

Ralph Morgan: important organizer and rule maker

James Naismith: inventor of basketball

Harold G. Olsen: helped create NCAA tournament

Original Celtics: best team of the 1920s

John J. Schomer: three-time All-America at Chicago

Amos Alonzo Stagg: longtime coach (of football, too!)

Oswald Tower: referee and rulesmaker

NEW MEMBERS

Here's the 2010 Class of inductees, bringing the total to 293 members of the Hall of Fame.

1960 UNITED STATES OLYMPIC TEAM
Won gold medal, swamping opponents

1992 UNITED STATES OLYMPIC TEAM
Won gold medal; first team with pros

JERRY BUSS
Lakers owner with eight NBA championship rings

CYNTHIA COOPER-DYKE
College and WNBA star

BOB HURLEY SR.
Longtime high school coach

DENNIS JOHNSON
Five-time NBA All-Star guard

GUS JOHNSON
High-scoring NBA power forward

KARL MALONE ▶▶▶
Jazz great second all-time in scoring

MACIEL "UBIRATAN" PEREIRA
Brazilian star

SCOTTIE PIPPEN
Helped Bulls win six NBA titles

GOLDEN STATE
WARRIORS

Though their team's full name comes from the nickname of their home state, the Warriors have been golden only once, way back in 1975. However, some great new talent has things looking up in the Bay Area.

GAME 1?
1947

One of the league's most storied teams, the Warriors were in Philadelphia from 1947–62. From 1963–71, they played in San Francisco. They became Golden State in 1971.

MAGIC MOMENT
1975 NBA Finals

Talented forward Rick Barry helped the Warriors lead the NBA in scoring and win their third NBA championship.

LOWEST LOW
2000–01 Season

The "lowlight" of the Warriors' 12-season run of losing seasons (1995–2006) was a sorry 65-loss season in 2000–01.

STUFF

HOME:
Oracle Arena

NBA TITLES: 3

ONLY IN OAKLAND:
The team used to have a mascot named Thunder. Then the new Oklahoma City team chose that as its nickname!

STAR SEASONS!

1953
The first great scoring threat for the Warriors was Neil Johnston, who won the first of his three NBA points titles.

1992
Golden State's Don Nelson was named the NBA Coach of the Year after leading the team to 55 victories.

1994
Former Michigan star Chris Webber was named the NBA's Rookie of the year.

WILT CHAMBERLAIN

He only played his first five-and-a-half seasons with the Warriors, but wow, . . . those were some seasons! "The Stilt" led the NBA in scoring and rebounding from 1959–60 through 1962–63, then scoring alone for two more years after that. His 50.4 points per game in 1961–62 is a record.

#1

FUNKY FACTS

➜ In 1946, the Philadelphia Warriors were the first champions of the Basketball Association of America, one of the groups that later formed today's NBA.

➜ Wilt Chamberlain was with the Philadelphia Warriors in 1962 when he scored an NBA-record 100 points in a game.

➜ The Warriors have been home to both the tallest and shortest NBA players in history: center Manute Bol (tied for tallest at 7-7) and guard Muggsy Bogues at 5-3. Bol, a native of Sudan, was also the only player in NBA history to block more shots than he made. He swatted about 2,086 shots but only

SUPERSTAR!
MONTA ELLIS

Ellis excels on offense and defense for the Warriors. He's among the best in the league at making steals, and in 2009–10, he finished fifth in the league with a 25.5 points per game average.

made a total of 1,599 over the course of his career!

➜ The Warriors are the only NBA team without a state or city in their name. Golden State is a nickname for California.

You Can Look It Up! GOLDEN STATE'S OFFICIAL WEBSITE: www.nba.com/warriors.com

LOS ANGELES
CLIPPERS

The Clippers have had several homes, but have not brought home an NBA title to any of them. Playing for most of that time in the shadow of the Lakers, the Clips, as they are called, always face an upcourt struggle.

GAME 1?
1971

The Clippers started way back East as the Buffalo Braves. They moved to San Diego in 1978 and changed to their current name. They made the move to L.A. in 1984.

MAGIC MOMENT
Best One Yet!

With a solid 47 wins and a spot in the Western Conference semis, the 2006 Clippers had their best season in a long time.

LOWEST LOW
Team Refund!

So many to choose from, unfortunately. A 70-loss campaign in 1987 was the worst full season, however.

STUFF

HOME:
Staples Center

NBA TITLES: 0

ONLY IN L.A.:
As the only NBA teams to share an arena, the Lakers and Clippers take turns as the "home" team for their matchups.

STAR SEASONS!

1974 Big Bob McAdoo won the first of his three straight NBA scoring titles while starring for the then-Buffalo Braves.

1974 Flashy point guard Ernie DiGregorio led the NBA in assists, dishing out 8.2 per game to Braves teammates.

1988 Center Michael Cage led the NBA in rebounding, averaging 13 boards per game.

The Ultimate Clipper

RANDY SMITH

Straddling the Braves and Clippers eras, Smith used his frontcourt skills to set franchise career records for points, assists, and steals. A durable player who didn't miss a game for 10 seasons, he was a two-time All-Star and the 1978 All-Star MVP. He also spent time with the Knicks and Cavs in a career that ended in 1983.

#1

FUNKY FACTS

➜ The only NBA MVP in team history came in 1975, when high-scoring forward Bob McAdoo took home the trophy.

➜ Following each season, the NBA's non-playoff teams enter the NBA draft lottery to see who gets first pick. The Clippers have had 21 but only one (Danny Manning) has became an NBA All-Star.

➜ Michael Olowokandi, the Clippers' No. 1 Draft pick in 1998, was nicknamed "The Kandi Man."

➜ Longtime Clippers broadcaster Ralph Lawler is famous for "Lawler's Law," which states that the first team to make it to

100 points will win the game. Since 1978, the law has been true 91.5% of the time.

SUPERSTAR!
CHRIS KAMEN

In his seventh season with the Clippers, Kamen crashes his big 7-0 body into the paint for tons of rebounds. He was a 2010 NBA All-Star and has been among league leaders in both boards and blocks.

LOS ANGELES LAKERS

In both of the team's homes, the Lakers have been champions. With 16 NBA titles, the Lakers trail only the Boston Celtics—whom they beat for the title in 2010! The Lakers have featured some of the NBA's greatest players.

GAME 1?
1948

The team was born in Minneapolis, known as "Land of 10,000 Lakes." When they moved to L.A. for the 1961 season, they kept the name, even though Los Angeles is lake-free!

 ## MAGIC MOMENT
2010 NBA Finals

The Lakers won a Game 7 against their archrivals, the Celtics, for the first time in the rivalry's storied history.

LOWEST LOW
1957–58 Season

The Lakers plummeted to last place, winning only 19 games, after making the playoffs in each of their first nine seasons.

STUFF

HOME:
Staples Center

NBA TITLES: 16

ONLY IN L.A.:
Courtside seats at Lakers games are regularly filled with some of the biggest celebrities in movies, TV, and music.

STAR SEASONS!

1949 In the first season of pro basketball, the Lakers proved to be the best in the land, winning their first league championship.

1972 On their way to another NBA title, the Lakers set an NBA record by winning 33 games in a row.

2002 The Lakers won their third straight NBA title, their first "three-peat" since 1954.

MAGIC JOHNSON

Bursting into the league in 1979 with a huge smile and an even bigger game, Earvin "Magic" Johnson set a new standard for point guards, while also establishing a new, boyish leadership. He helped the Lakers win five NBA titles and was a three-time Finals MVP. Magic retired in 1992 after revealing he had HIV.

#1

FUNKY FACTS

➡ Lakers star George Mikan was the first "big man" in the NBA. He led the league in scoring in its first three years, while helping the Lakers win five NBA titles in his seven seasons.

➡ Famed Lakers guard Jerry West had such perfect form, his silohuette forms the NBA logo of a player dribbling with his left hand.

➡ The Lakers' exciting offense in the 1980s was known by the nickname "Showtime."

➡ When Shaquille O'Neal was with the Lakers from 1996–2004, his nicknames included "Shaq Daddy," "Big Diesel," and "Big Aristotle."

SUPERSTAR! KOBE BRYANT

Called by many the best player in the NBA, Kobe started with the Lakers when he was just 18. A four-time NBA points leader, he has helped L.A. win five NBA titles, including in 2010.

➡ The Lakers have been owned since 1979 by Dr. Jerry Buss. He's not a medical doctor, though. He got his degree in physical chemistry.

You Can Look It Up! L.A.'S OFFICIAL WEBSITE: www.nba.com/lakers.com

PHOENIX SUNS

So close and still no trophy. The Suns have missed the playoffs only three times since 1988 and have featured a host of amazing athletes. Their loyal fans will stick with them until they can finally break through to the top!

GAME 1?
1968

The Suns rose (get it?!) as an expansion team in 1968. By their second season, they were in the playoffs; by their eighth they had made the NBA Finals!

👍 MAGIC MOMENT
The Suns Rise!

The Suns set a team record with 62 wins and won their only Western Conference title, before falling in the Finals to the Bulls.

👎 LOWEST LOW
Bad Beginning

With such a long record of success, you have to go back to the Sun's first season, a 66-loss slow start in 1968–69.

STUFF

HOME:
US Airways Center

NBA TITLES: 0

ONLY IN PHOENIX:
To honor the many Hispanic fans in their home state, the team sometimes sports jerseys that read "Los Suns."

STAR SEASONS!

1989
Phoenix coach Cotton Fitzsimmons won the Red Auerbach Award as NBA coach of the year.

2006
Leandro Barbosa won the NBA's Sixth Man award as the league's top subsitute.

2010
Superstar guard Steve Nash led the NBA in both assists per game and free-throw percentage.

The Ultimate Sun

STEVE NASH

He could also be the Superstar, but his long career makes him an Ultimate. Nash won the first of his two NBA MVP awards in 2005, the first Canadian to win that honor. He also led the NBA in assists three times and free-throw percentage twice. A dashing, slashing perfect point guard, Nash is a surefire Hall of Famer.

#1

FUNKY FACTS

→ The team's owner since its first season is Jerry Colangelo. He was only 27 years old when he was granted an expansion team for Arizona; he also picked the team's name!

→ Superstar guard Steve Nash grew up playing soccer. He got a chance to show off his skills during the 2005 NBA Slam Dunk Contest. He headed the ball in the air for teammate Amar'e Stoudemire to slam home!

→ The Suns got their famous Gorilla mascot by accident. In 1979, a fan sent a telegram singer in a gorilla suit. After delivering his message, he stayed and entertained fans. Soon, he was offered a full-time job!

SUPERSTAR!

JASON RICHARDSON

How's this for an all-around talent? Not only has Richardson led the NBA in three-point shots made, he's also a regular at the annual NBA Slam Dunk Contest on All-Star weekend!

→ The first regular season NBA games played outside the United States took place in Tokyo, Japan, when the Suns matched up against the Jazz twice to open the 1990-91 season.

You Can Look It Up! PHOENIX'S OFFICIAL WEBSITE: www.nba.com/suns.com

SACRAMENTO KINGS

One of the NBA's most well-traveled franchises, the Kings have found a long-time home in "Sacto," where they have found some of the NBA's loudest and most loyal fans. No titles there yet, but they have the talent to make it happen.

GAME 1?
1948

The Rochester (N.Y.) Royals were part of the BAA that helped form the NBA. From there they moved to Cincinnati, Kansas City-Omaha, and finally Sacramento in 1985.

MAGIC MOMENT
Long Time Ago

As the Kings, they've had some good seasons, but the franchise's only NBA title came in Rochester in 1951.

LOWEST LOW
Highs and Lows

The Kings followed a string of eight playoff teams with four losing seasons, the worst of which was 65 losses in 2008–09.

STUFF

HOME:

ARCO Arena

NBA TITLES: 1

ONLY IN SACRAMENTO:

The Kings have a mascot who's the king of beasts. Slamson the Lion gets some serious "hair" on dunks.

STAR SEASONS!

1964 Oscar Robertson, as a member of the Cincinnati Royals, won the NBA MVP award.

1973 Point guard Nate "Tiny" Archibald was the NBA assists leader while the team played in Kansas City and Omaha.

1975 The team was known as the Kansas City-Omaha Kings when Phil Johnson was named the NBA's coach of the year.

OSCAR ROBERTSON

He was actually never a King, only a Royal, but he was the still the best. "The Big O" is one of the most talented all-around players ever. He's the only man to average a triple double for a season (1961–62), was a Rookie of the Year and an NBA MVP, led the leauge in assists seven times, and was an 11-time All-NBA pick.

#1

FUNKY FACTS

➔ In 1945, Otto Graham led the Rochester Royals to the National Basketball League title. He later switched sports, playing quarterback for the Cleveland Browns and helping them win seven league championships.

➔ The great Celtics guard Bob Cousy made his only stab at coaching in the NBA with the Royals, leading the team from 1969–73. Another Celtics great, Bill Russell, came out of retirement to run Sacramento for the 1987–88 season.

➔ Why Kings? What's another way to say what sort of person a king is? A "royal."

➔ Forward Omar Casspi

SUPERSTAR! TYREKE EVANS

The 2010 NBA Rookie of the Year looks to be a backcourt fixture in Sacramento for years. A talented passer who leads the team's offense, he can also score using a solid outside shot.

became the first NBA player form Israel when he debuted for the Kings in 2009.

➔ The Kings are owned by a pair of high-flying brothers: Gavin and Joe Maloof.

You Can Look It Up! SACRAMENTO'S OFFICIAL WEBSITE: www.nba.com/kings.com

OVERTIME

We ran out of quarters, but not out of basketball stuff. Here's where put all the topics that didn't fit anywhere else: champions of the pros and college, the Olympic basketball story, the All-Star Game, wheelchair hoops, pickup games, and more!

INSIDE:

Michael Jordan (23) won six NBA championships with Chicago.

NBA CHAMPS!

SEASON	TEAM	SEASON	TEAM
1946–47*	Philadelphia Warriors	1965–66	Boston Celtics
1947–48*	Baltimore Bullets	1966–67	Philadelphia 76ers
1948–49	Minneapolis Lakers	1967–68	Boston Celtics
1949–50	Minneapolis Lakers	1968–69	Boston Celtics
1950–51	Rochester Royals	1969–70	New York Knicks
1951–52	Minneapolis Lakers	1970–71	Milwaukee Bucks
1952–53	Minneapolis Lakers	1971–72	L.A. Lakers
1953–54	Minneapolis Lakers	1972–73	New York Knicks
1954–55	Syracuse Nationals	1973–74	Boston Celtics
1955–56	Philadelphia Warriors	1974–75	Golden State Warriors
1956–57	Boston Celtics	1975–76	Boston Celtics
1957–58	St. Louis Hawks	1976–77	Portland Trail Blazers
1958–59	Boston Celtics	1977–78	Washington Bullets
1959–60	Boston Celtics	1978–79	Seattle Supersonics
1960–61	Boston Celtics	1979–80	L.A. Lakers
1961–62	Boston Celtics	1980–81	Boston Celtics
1962–63	Boston Celtics	1981–82	L.A. Lakers
1963–64	Boston Celtics	1982–83	Philadelphia 76ers
1964–65	Boston Celtics	1983–84	Boston Celtics

SEASON	TEAM
1984-85	L.A. Lakers
1985-86	Boston Celtics
1986-87	L.A. Lakers
1987-88	L.A. Lakers
1988-89	Detroit Pistons
1989-90	Detroit Pistons
1990-91	Chicago Bulls
1991-92	Chicago Bulls
1992-93	Chicago Bulls
1993-94	Houston Rockets
1994-95	Houston Rockets
1995-96	Chicago Bulls
1996-97	Chicago Bulls
1997-98	Chicago Bulls
1998-99	San Antonio Spurs
1999-00	L.A. Lakers
2000-01	L.A. Lakers
2001-02	L.A. Lakers
2002-03	San Antonio Spurs
2003-04	Detroit Pistons
2004-05	San Antonio Spurs
2005-06	Miami Heat

2010 NBA Champions: Kobe Bryant and the L.A. Lakers

SEASON	TEAM
2006-07	San Antonio Spurs
2007-08	Boston Celtics
2008-09	L.A. Lakers
2009-10	L.A. Lakers
2010-11	_____

*BAA Champions; see page 16.

NBA FINALS
GREAT MOMENTS

The NBA Finals are always jam-packed with big plays, amazing shots, stunning turnarounds, and surprising stars. We could fill a whole book with great events from the more than 60 years of NBA Finals, but we had to pick just a few.

1969 Russell's Last One

The greatest champion in NBA history went out on a high note. Bill Russell led the Celtics to their 11th title since he joined the team in 1956. The last three of those, he was the player-coach, the first African-American to hold that role in any major American sport.

1970 West's Amazing Shot

Though it came in what ended as a loss, Jerry West's buzzer-beating, game-tying, 60-foot shot in Game 3 remains one of the most famous in Finals history. It tied the game, but the Knicks won in overtime.

1970 Willis Reed's Return

He only scored four points in the game, but his presence thrilled his team. Willie Reed was expected to miss Game 7 with a torn thigh muscle. But to the cheers of the hometown Madison Square Garden crowd, he limped onto the court to start the game. After two baskets, he came out, unable to run. But his courage inspired his team win their first NBA title.

1980 Dr. J's Swoop

Though his team lost to the Lakers in six games, Julius "Dr. J" Erving made an unforgettable play in Game 4. Leaping toward the basket from one side of the key, he somehow ended up laying the ball in from the other side of the hoop! It was a miracle shot by a miracle-worker.

1980 Magic's Baby Hook

With star center Kareem Abdul-Jabbar out for Game 6, rookie guard Magic Johnson put the Lakers on his shoulders and led them to victory. Using a Kareem-inspired "baby hook" shot, Magic scored 42 points and had 15 rebounds and his first NBA championship ring.

1991 Jordan's First

The start of something big: Michael Jordan, already a superstar and scoring champ, earned his first NBA championship.

1998 Jordan's Last ▶

Michael Jordan capped off one of sports' greatest careers by single-handedly winning Game 6. Down by three with less than a minute to go, Jordan made a layup, a steal, and a title-winning shot. He had 45 points on the way to his sixth NBA Finals MVP and the Bulls' sixth title.

2010 Lakers Top Celtics

In only the second Game 7 in an NBA Finals since 1994, a clutch shot by Derek Fisher kicked off an 11–0 run by the Lakers. They won their second straight title by defeating archrival Boston 83–79. The championship put the Lakers just one behind the Celtics' 17 overall NBA titles.

NCAA MEN'S
CHAMPIONS

2011	_____	2004	**Connecticut**
2010	**Duke**	2003	**Syracuse**
2009	**North Carolina**	2002	**Maryland**
2008	**Kansas**	2001	**Duke**
2007	**Florida**	2000	**Michigan State**
2006	**Florida**	1999	**Connecticut**
2005	**North Carolina**	1998	**Kentucky**

Coach Mike Krzyzewski (left) accepts Duke's 2010 NCAA title trophy.

1997	**Arizona**	1967	**UCLA**
1996	**Kentucky**	1966	**Texas Western**
1995	**UCLA**	1965	**UCLA**
1994	**Arkansas**	1964	**UCLA**
1993	**North Carolina**	1963	**Loyola (Illinois)**
1992	**Duke**	1962	**Cincinnati**
1991	**Duke**	1961	**Cincinnati**
1990	**UNLV**	1960	**Ohio State**
1989	**Michigan**	1959	**California**
1988	**Kansas**	1958	**Kentucky**
1987	**Indiana**	1957	**North Carolina**
1986	**Louisville**	1956	**San Francisco**
1985	**Villanova**	1955	**San Francisco**
1984	**Georgetown**	1954	**La Salle**
1983	**NC State**	1953	**Indiana**
1982	**North Carolina**	1952	**Kansas**
1981	**Indiana**	1951	**Kentucky**
1980	**Louisville**	1950	**City Coll. of N.Y.**
1979	**Michigan State**	1949	**Kentucky**
1978	**Kentucky**	1948	**Kentucky**
1977	**Marquette**	1947	**Holy Cross**
1976	**Indiana**	1946	**Oklahoma A & M**
1975	**UCLA**	1945	**Oklahoma A & M**
1974	**NC State**	1944	**Utah**
1973	**UCLA**	1943	**Wyoming**
1972	**UCLA**	1942	**Stanford**
1971	**UCLA**	1941	**Wisconsin**
1970	**UCLA**	1940	**Indiana**
1969	**UCLA**	1939	**Oregon**
1968	**UCLA**		

FINAL FOURS

The annual men's national college basketball championship ends with the "Final Four": two semifinals and the national final. The games draw huge TV audiences and often include dramatic and memorable moments. Here are a few of those moments.

1957 TWO TRIPLE OTS

North Carolina needed three overtimes to beat Michigan in a semifinal. It needed three more to knock off Kansas, led by the great Wilt Chamberlain. The Tar Heels ended up with a perfect 32–0 record for their first national title.

1966 A CIVIL RIGHTS BREAKTHROUGH

Though fans of today's game might be surprised, African-American players were still somewhat rare in college basketball in the early 1960s. In 1966, Texas Western (now called UTEP) was the first to field an all-black starting lineup. To the dismay of teams from the South, Texas Western made the national final. There they beat an all-white team from Kentucky.

1973 NEAR-PERFECTION

Center Bill Walton made 21 of his 22 shots, leading UCLA to the ninth of the 10 titles it would win under legendary coach John Wooden. A tenth title in 1975 wrapped up a decade-plus of dominance for Wooden and the Bruins.

1983 JIMMY V!

Highly-favored Houston lost on a last-second

SCORING HEROES

Here are the highest single-game scoring performances in Final Four history.

POINTS	PLAYER	SCHOOL	YEAR
61	Austin Carr	Notre Dame	1970
58	Bill Bradley	Princeton	1965
56	Oscar Robertson	Cincinnati	1958
52	Austin Carr	Notre Dame	1970
52	Austin Carr	Notre Dame	1971

slam dunk by North Carolina State's Lorenzo Charles. NC State coach Jimmy Valvano's excited dash around the court became a video legend. His early death from cancer in 1993 saddened the sport.

1979 MAGIC VS. BIRD

Two of basketball's greatest players started their career-long rivalry in this game. Indiana State's Larry Bird met Michigan State's Magic Johnson in the final game. The contest drew the highest TV ratings of any college hoops game ever. The two stars did not disappoint their fans, putting on a great display of basketball. Magic's Spartans won 75–64.

1985 SUPER UPSET!

Led by the mighty Patrick Ewing, most people thought No. 1 Georgetown was a shoo-in for the title. In the final, however, their Big East rivals from Villanova shocked the basketball world. 'Nova's 66–64 upset made them the only No. 8 seed to win the national title.

1991 SWEET REVENGE

In 1990, Duke had been stunned to lose the NCAA championship game to the University of Nevada/Las Vegas by 30 points. In 1991, they got back at UNLV, beating them in the rematch.

1993 THE TIMEOUT, NOT!

Michigan star Chris Webber had the ball with 11 seconds left. His team trailed North Carolina by two. He had a chance to be the hero. Then he called timeout. Oops. By calling a TO when he team was out of them, he gave the Tar Heels free throws, the ball, and the championship.

2010 HEYWARD'S HEAVE ▶▶▶

The surprising Butler Bulldogs beat team after team in dramatic fashion on their way to meeting Duke in the final game. Near the game's end, they trailed by two. On the final play, Butler's Gordon Heyward just missed a halfcourt shot that would have won the game!

NBA
ALL-STAR GAME

When the best NBA stars get together, defense goes out the window! The annual NBA All-Star Game, usually held midseason in February, pits the best in the Western Conference against the best in the Eastern. Since the game doesn't count for much, both teams go all-out to put on an offensive show of amazing shots, super slams, and highlight-reel passes. Here's a quick look at some memorable All-Star moments.

1983: Showstarter The biggest moment of this night came when singer Marvin Gaye gave one of the most amazing performances of the National Anthem ever heard before or since.

1988: The MJ Show First, Michael Jordan won the Slam Dunk contest, taking off from the free throw line! Then he poured in 40 points to win the game MVP award. Wow!

1992: Magic and Tears Beloved Lakers guard Magic Johnson was leaving the sport he loved after he got the virus that causes AIDS. In what was going to be his final moment in hoops, he played most of the All-Star Game, scored 25 points including a jumper at the buzzer, and was the game's MVP.

2001: The Comeback The East trailed by 21 points, but led by Allen Iverson playing in front of his hometown Philly fans, came back to win by one point.

2003: Let's Keep Playing! In the highest-scoring game in All-Star history, the West needed two overtimes to win 155–145.

2008: A King Flies LeBron James put the East ahead to stay by soaring over 7-foot Dirk Nowitzki to throw down a thunderous dunk.

SLAMMMMM
DUNK!

One of the most popular events on the NBA calendar is the Slam Dunk Contest. Held the day before the NBA All-Star Game, it pits the most creative, high-flying, backboard-rattling, rim-shaking dunkers in the league. They can do just about anything they want as long the ball whams through the net! Players have used props, capes, blindfolds, teammates, costumes, and more. Judges and an adoring crowd decide the winners. Here's a list of the top dunkers from past events (not held in 1998–99).

YEAR SLAM DUNK CHAMP, TEAM

2010 **Nate ROBINSON,** Knicks

2009 **Nate ROBINSON,** Knicks

2008 **Dwight HOWARD,** Magic

2007 **Gerald GREEN,** Celtics

2006 **Nate ROBINSON,** Knicks

2005 **Josh SMITH,** Hawks

2004 **Fred JONES,** Pacers

2003 **Jason RICHARDSON,** Warriors

2002 **Jason RICHARDSON,** Warriors

2001 **Desmond MASON,** Supersonics

2000 **Vince CARTER,** Raptors

1997 **Kobe BRYANT,** Lakers

1996 **Brent BARRY,** Clippers

1995 **Harold MINER,** Heat

1994 **Isaiah RIDER,** Timberwolves

1993 **Harold MINER,** Cavaliers

1992 **Cedric CEBALLOS,** Suns

1991 **Dee BROWN,** Celtics

1990 **Dominique WILKINS,** Hawks

1989 **Kenny WALKER,** Knicks

Dwight "Superman" Howard in 2008

YEAR SLAM DUNK CHAMP, TEAM

1988 **Michael JORDAN,** Bulls

1987 **Michael JORDAN,** Bulls

1986 **Spud WEBB,** Hawks

1985 **Dominique WILKINS,** Hawks

1984 **Larry NANCE,** Suns

OLYMPIC
HOOPS

Basketball has been part of the Olympics since 1936. That year, the final was played on a court made of sand . . . in the rain! The squishy court made for a really sloppy game, but the U.S. team beat Canada 19–8 to win the first hoops gold medal. World War II interrupted the Games until 1948. The U.S. went on a dominant win streak, winning every game they played and every gold medal . . . until 1972 (see note below). The sport has grown enormously around the world and today the Olympic tournament features several outstanding teams. Here are some Olympic highlights.

Soviet star Alexander Belov makes the winning layup in 1972.

1960 team
A U.S. team led by future NBA stars Oscar Robertson, Jerry West, and Jerry Lucas dominated the competition. It won most of their games by 40 or more points. In the final, they beat Brazil 90–63: a squeaker! In 2010, the entire team was named to the Basketball Hall of Fame.

1972 US–Soviet Battle
In the wildest ending to a basketball game ever, the USSR beat the U.S. 51–50. The U.S. led 50–49 and then time seemed to have run out. The U.S. team celebrated, thinking the game was over. The referees, however, first put two seconds back on the clock, then put three seconds. The "re-do" gave the Soviets two more chances to bring the ball back in . . . for reasons that remain very murky. The USSR made a layup amid a confused U.S. team and earned a tainted gold medal.

1976 First Women's Tournament Finally!
Women got their first Olympic tournament 40 years after the first men's event. The USSR team beat a strong U.S. team in the final.

1992 Dream Team In an effort to get the big stars of
the NBA (and other countries' pro leagues) into the Olympics, pros were allowed starting in 1992 (previously, only U.S. college players were on the team). The U.S. made up a "Dream Team" that brought home the gold. Among the members: Larry Bird, Michael Jordan, Magic Johnson, Karl Malone, and Charles Barkley. It was a Bad Dream for other countries!

2004 Argentina? The U.S. dominance of Olympic
basketball only increased with the coming of the pros. However, in 2004, the rest of the world finally got the better of the Americans. The U.S team squeaked out of the first round, losing their first two non-medal games ever. In a semifinal, they lost to Argentina, stunning the hoops world. The Argentines were led by Spurs star Manu Ginobili; the U.S. settled for bronze.

Olympic Champions

MEN

2008	USA	1984	USA	1960	USA
2004	Argentina	1980*	Yugoslavia	1956	USA
2000	USA	1976	USA	1952	USA
1996	USA	1972	USSR	1948	USA
1992	USA	1968	USA	1936	USA
1988	USSR	1964	USA		

WOMEN

2008	USA	1996	USA	1984	USA
2004	USA	1992	Unified Team**	1980*	USSR
2000	USA	1988	USA	1976	USSR

*In 1980, the United States boycotted—did not attend—the Summer Games in Moscow in protest of the Soviet Union's invasion of Afghanistan.

**The Unified Team was made up of players from countries that had recently been part of the Soviet Union, which was breaking up in the early 1990s.

WHEELCHAIR
BASKETBALL

Unlike some major sports, basketball can be adapted so that disabled people can take part easily. In wheelchair basketball, the game is pretty much the same . . . but without jumping or slam dunks. Players roll on a full-sized court, dribbling, passing, and shooting. Here are some facts about wheelchair basketball that you probably didn't know!

➡ The sport was first played by injured veterans after their return from World War II.

➡ The first women's team was formed at the University of Illinois in 1970.

➡ The sport has been in the Paralympics since 1960. In 2008, Australia won the men's event, while the United States won the women's (photo).

➡ Official wheelchairs can only be 21 inches high at the seat. The wheels are usually tilted out at the bottom to make turning and balance easier.

➡ Wheelchair basketball is played by college teams and company teams around the country.

➡ A world championship is also held, with past champions hailing from Israel, the Netherlands, France, and the United States.

➡ To dribble in wheelchair hoops, a player must make one bounce for every two turns of the wheel. There is also no double dribbling. Players also can pivot as in regular hoops, but must stay in one place while doing so. And players can't tilt their chairs onto footrests to gain an advantage. Otherwise, it's pretty much basketball as usual.

PICKUP

BASKETBALL

Have your heard the phrase "unwritten rules"? These are things that are understood to be the way things work in a sport or a job, but aren't really written in a rulebook. Well, we're going to write some of those down! Pickup basketball is the way that most kids start playing the game. Adults play it a lot, too, on courts big and small around the world. To join a game, you need to know how it's played. Here's a quick sample of the key "rules."

Shooter keeps it:
During warmups, a shooter who makes his shot gets the ball back . . . until he or she misses!

Take it back:
During a game, the ball has to be dribbled or passed past a certain line each time possession changes.

Check:
After each basket, the defense gets the ball for a moment until they are ready to start again; they then give it to the offense.

Call your own fouls:
You're in charge of calling fouls committed against you.

Winners:
You make a basket, you keep the ball. You win the game, you stay on the court.

We got next:
What you say to determine what team will play the winners next.

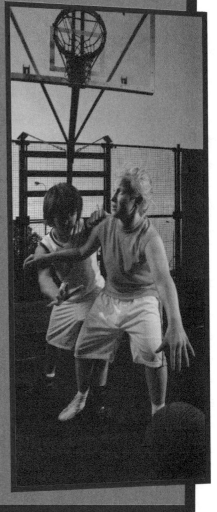

BASKETBALL RULES QUIZ

Time to test your knowledge of how basketball is played. See if you can come up with the right answer to these questions about the rules of the game.

1 A defensive player grabs a shot just as it is about to go into the hoop. What does the ref call?

2 A point guard dribbles down the court and then stops dribbling. He holds the ball for a moment . . . then starts dribbling again; what's the call?

3 A shot bounces high off the rim and goes behind the backboard, where an offensive player grabs it. Can he shoot again?

4 A player in-bounds the ball to a teammate who stuffs home a basket. However, the player making the pass stepped on the sideline as he made the pass. Does the basket count?

5 A player makes a long pass that bounces off his teammate's head . . . and into the basket. Does the shot count?

6 With less than a second left, a player leaps and shoots. As the ball is flying toward the basket, the buzzer sounds, ending the game. If the ball goes in, does the shot count?

7 While playing defense, a player reaches out with his foot and deflects a pass. It goes to a teammate, who dribbles in to shoot. Is this a fair play?

Answers: 1. Goaltending, basket counts; 2. Double dribble; 3. No, once a ball goes up and over the backboard, it's out of play; 4. No, the ref should rule the pass no good; you can't step on the line while putting the ball back in play; 5. Yes, no matter how the ball goes in, it counts as a made shot; 6. Yes, as long as the ball leaves the player's hand before the buzzer, the shot counts; 7. No, a player may not kick the ball on purpose; the other team keeps possession.

FIND OUT MORE

We couldn't fit everything about basketball in this book. It would have been 900 pages long! There's lots more about the game, its players, its teams, and its history that you can track down. Here are a few books and Web sites that you can visit to find out more about hoops!

WEB SITES

www.nba.com
The official site of the NBA is packed with stats, bios, news, and video galore. Read about the league's history and check in with the biggest stars.

www.basketball-reference.com
Like stats? Then this is the place for you. You can dive into this site and find just about anything. They also have all-time leaders in dozens of categories and complete stats of thousands of players.

www.ncaa.com/sports/m-baskbl
www.ncaa.com/sports/w-baskbl
These two sites take you to the home of men's and women's college hoops. Check out the standings in all the conferences and get ready for the craziness of the tournaments.

BOOKS

EYEWITNESS BASKETBALL
By John Hareas (2005, DK)
From the first 24-second clock to NBA.com, this picture-packed book covers every part of basketball—play diagrams, stories of the game's greats, memorabilia from the NBA Finals, and much more.

LAST SHOT:
A FINAL FOUR MYSTERY
By John Feinstein (2006, Yearling Books)
A top sportswriter created this basketball-themed mystery for young readers. It's a different way to dive into your favorite sport, as you help young detectives try to stop crime amid the college playoffs.

GLOSSARY

barnstormer   a player or team that travels great distances, playing in athletic events in each place they stop

clutch   coming through when your team needs you most

contribute   add to the total of something

defunct   no longer playing or no longer existing

dominance   overwhelming force; very successful for a long time

employee   a person who works for a company

gracious   thoughtful, pleasant, complimentary

inflate   add air to

innovative   groundbreaking, inventive, creative

intimidating   causing fear or worry due to size or strength

salary   money paid on a regular schedule to a person performing work

springs   basketball slang for great leaping ability

INDEX

THE LONG & SHORT OF IT

Here's a list of the tallest and shortest players in NBA history. As you can see, it takes all sizes to make a great pro basketball player.

HEIGHT FT-IN (M)	PLAYER
7-7 (2.31)	Manute Bol
	Gheorge Muresan
7-6 (2.28)	Yao Ming*
	Shawn Bradley
7-5 (2.26)	Chuck Nevitt
	Slavko Vranes
7-4 (2.23)	Mark Eaton
	Rik Smits
	Ralph Sampson
	Priest Lauderdale
5-3 (1.60)	Muggsy Bogues
5-5 (1.65)	Earl Boykins*
5-7 (1.70)	Spud Webb
	Wataru Misaka
5-9 (1.75)	Nate Robinson
	Calvin Murphy
5-10 (1.77)	Michael Adams
	Avery Johnson

*Active through 2009–10